INVISIBLE
NEIGHBORS

JOHN ASHMEN

Thanks to Emily Blake for her cover photo and
some additional inside photography.
(http://emily-lauren-blake.tumblr.com/)

First Printing: August 2011

Unless indicated otherwise, Scripture quotations
are from the Holy Bible, New International Version,
copyright © 1973, 1978, 1984 by International Bible
Society.

Printed in the United States of America

CROSS SECTION
940 CALLE NEGOCIO, SUITE 175
SAN CLEMENTE, CALIFORNIA 92673
www.InvisibleNeighbors.org
www.Crosssection.com
www.LoudToast.com
www.MissionPrint.com
www.TheGospelQuest.com

During the preparation of this resource, all citations, facts, figures, names,
addresses, telephone numbers, Internet URLs, and other cited information
were verified for accuracy. Cross Section has made every attempt to reference current and valid sources, but we cannot guarantee the content of any
source and we are not responsible for any changes that may have occurred
since our verification. If you find an error in, or have a question or concern
about, any of the information or sources listed within, please contact us
at info@crosssection.com. Any individual represented in a photo or video
for Invisible Neighbors are not intended to imply that they are homeless,
abused or addicted.

## Acknowledgements

Alison Phillips
Bill Nash
Bob Wenz
Dan Peddie
David Harms
Doug Martinez
Emily Blake
Gail Engstrom
Jack Yearwood
Jason Pearson
Jesse Ashmen
John Pearson
Judi Ashmen
Kris Hull
Lily Wright
Mike Yankoski
Nicole Daniels
Nicole Peña
Rhett Butler

## Welcome

If you're looking for an inspiring devotional or an uplifting Bible study, this isn't it. *Invisible Neighbors* is a pointed publication with relevant media accompaniments that delves into our most serious and growing social issues in North America. And in doing so, it clearly explains the mandate for followers of Jesus.

The author blends captivating narratives, enlightening history lessons, and current events, cementing them together with important biblical perspectives. Each teaching unit has questions that prompt you to share feelings and viewpoints, or help develop stances based on God's truth. Prepare to be challenged and forced out of your comfort zone.

*Invisible Neighbors*, which can be broken down into six or 18 sections, is designed for a small-group study. It's ideal for adult home groups, college and career groups, youth groups, and more. But it will also deliver maximum impact if you simply read it on your own.

God bless you as you pour over *Invisible Neighbors*. And may it affect you greatly.

*Here is a brief explanation of the features in the study guide:*

## ENGAGE
There is a video lesson for the group to watch together each week. Take notes in the spaces provided as you watch the DVD and be sure to refer back to those notes during the group discussion time. Each video segment is complemented by corresponding questions for group discussion. Give everyone who wants to share the opportunity to do so and don't feel like you need to rush through all of the questions.

## CONNECT
You will open each meeting with an opportunity for everyone to connect with each other. The questions are designed to get conversation going and learn more about the lives of the members of your group. Give anyone who wants to share ample time and don't feel rushed to get through them all. It's okay if you don't answer all the questions!

## GO DEEPER
We are not called to be just hearers of the Word; we are called to be doers of the Word (James 1:22). This section of the study provides participants with exercises that will help put into practice the truths they have discussed in the lesson. Depending on time, this section can be completed during the group meeting or outside of the group on your own time.

## STUDY
Each section provides groups the opportunity to do further study on the topic. These Scripture passages and discussion questions are designed either for the group to discuss or for each individual to explore outside of the group on their own time. Don't feel pressured to spend time on every go deeper section during your group meeting. There may be some you want to focus on and some you don't. Feel the freedom to choose.

## GROW
This is the heart of the session. Ask group members to alternate reading the referenced Scripture passages and spend time discussing the corresponding questions. Don't feel pressured to discuss every single question. The material in the study is meant to help you gain a clear biblical perspective on the main theme of the session.

## PRAYER & PRAISE
At the end of each session you will be asked to spend time praying together as a group. A chart is provided that can be used to record prayer requests and praise reports. Praying together is one of the greatest privileges of small group life.

Engage: Watch Session One on video

# WHO IS MY NEIGHBOR?

## Part One: "Hey, We're Neighbors!"

It was Thursday afternoon and I was heading home early from work. Traffic on the Interstate was unusually light. With the window down and the radio up, a warm breeze and Cool Jazz were doing their part to distance me from another crazy day at the office.

My Acura TL departed the six-lane and rolled to the bottom of the off ramp just as the light at Blue Creek Road turned red. I lowered the volume on the radio. At that instant, peripheral vision prepared me for an unscheduled appointment: I looked to the left and our eyes met.

He was likely in his 40s, but the haggard face between a matted beard and tattered cap made him appear much older. Even if I closed my window my sunroof was fully open; an exchange of some kind with this homeless man was inevitable.

"Gorgeous day." His voice revealed his age and confirmed my suspicions.

"Sure is," seemed like the natural reply.

"Hot though," were his next words, as he did an obligatory scan of the cloudless sky.

"Yes, indeed."

A glance in my rearview mirror told me I would likely be his sole audience for the next 30 seconds or so.

"Heading home?" he asked, moving closer to the curb.

"I am," kept our two-word volley in play.

I tried to read his crude cardboard sign, but he was holding it off to the side at an awkward angle. This guy definitely needed a refresher class in roadside sales. The signal would soon be green and I'd be gone.

Expecting a pitch to come next, I scanned the console for quarters. Instead, he caught me off guard with a personal question.

"So what part of town you from?" Never breaking eye contact, he squatted down, took off his hat and wiped his forehead with a torn flannel sleeve. He seemed more interested in conversation than my loose change.

"I live in the Peregrine Hills area," I countered hesitantly, not wanting to be too specific.

His eyes widened and a broad smile rearranged the numerous wrinkles in his face. "Hey, we're neighbors! I live up behind you there on Pinion Ridge."

I tried to think of what houses were on Pinion Ridge; my internal GPS was only displaying boulders and bushes.

"Maybe I'll see you around sometime," he said, like we were old acquaintances running into each other at a downtown coffee shop. "The name's Charlie."

Long sullied nails pierced the air for the calloused fingers that followed. I leaned out and shook his extended hand.

"Do you need a ride home?"

Those six words hit me like barbs from a Taser. Who would ask such a reckless question? I turned to the passenger seat to find someone to blame. It held only my tightly zipped computer bag.

"If you don't mind, that would be great," Charlie answered tentatively, equally surprised by my offer. More at ease he added, "It'll take me an hour if I walk, and besides, things are pretty slow out here today."

Muttering a prayer for protection, I moved my laptop to the back seat and unlocked the front passenger door. Charlie climbed in and clicked his seatbelt right as the light turned green.

Over the next few miles I learned that my "neighbor" Charlie Goodall grew up in Ohio, raised by an abusive elderly aunt and a rebellious older sister. Suspended from high school in the 11th grade, he never reengaged with formal education. Since then, Charlie had lived in 12 states and held twice that number of jobs. Working as a Texas ranch hand was his favorite gig, but occasional stiff knees and regular stiff drinks had limited his current options.

With Pinion Ridge clearly in view, I asked Charlie where exactly he lived.

"Me and a few guys got a place yonder." The bill of his cap jerked to the west. I looked over at the rugged terrain and pulled to the shoulder.

"Do you have blankets?" I asked, knowing how cold it got in the upland at night.

"Yeah, we do fine. As good as all the others."

"What others?" was my question—one that pushed open a heavy door I didn't know was there.

Charlie went on to tell me that he knew of at least three dozen homeless people living within a few miles of my house: a bunch in the hills, some in culverts, a few in cars. He told me about someone called Chipshot who had managed to spend most of the summer sleeping in various crannies around the country club. He even worked himself in as a caddie on a few occasions, cleverly concealing his status from the duffers whose bags he toted.

I sat earnestly reflecting on my familiar surroundings. "I've never seen any of these people."

"That's because you're not looking," responded Charlie with an element of scorn. "We live right here among you but you go about in your bubble as if we didn't exist. We don't commute to work with you. We don't shop in your stores. We never make your dinner-party guest lists. We don't feel welcome in your churches. But we're still here. We're your neighbors…and we're growing in number."

After a few seconds of silence, Charlie thanked me for the ride and got out.

As I watched him stumble across the road and mount the steep path, I thought about my Christian faith and Jesus' instructions, both in light of this freshly concluded conversation.

"Charlie!" I got out and trotted his direction.

As I drew near, that same voice that had asked Charlie if he wanted a ride spoke again. This time I recognized it.

"We live at 4410 Kittredge Court. My wife and I talked about doing salmon on the backyard grill tomorrow night."

Charlie finger-combed his beard, waiting for my next words.

"There'll be plenty, Charlie. Can you join us?"

## CONNECT

What did you do the last time you encountered a homeless person at an intersection or on the street? What do you think is an appropriate response?

Was it foolhardy for the author to offer Charlie a ride? Under what circumstances would it be safe and fitting to do so?

How does Matthew 22:36-40 factor into this? What does loving your neighbor as yourself look like today?

How do you define neighbor? Is it disconcerting for you to hear someone say that the destitute in our midst might be our neighbors?

What are the stereotypes you have of homeless people, and how do you think they were formed? Who do you know that has a different perspective than you do on homelessness?

## GO DEEPER

Watch/listen to the "Do you have any place to stay tonight?" scene from the movie The Blind Side, and discuss it as a group.

# PART TWO: A CULTURE OF "COCOONS" AND "CLANS"

Harvard professor Robert Putnam wondered why there was such major demise in social capital throughout North America during the second half of the twentieth century. He looked around and asked: Why do Kiwanis and Rotary find it difficult to get younger members? Whatever happened to the ladies auxiliary down at the church? How is it you only hear about bridge clubs on black-and-white reruns? When was the last time there was a soapbox derby in town? Where have so many of the bowling leagues gone? And it wasn't just that these were antiquated activities; he noted that nothing else of any magnitude had risen up to draw in groups of divergent people for meaningful interaction.

Putnam turned his research into a book called Bowling Alone (Touchstone, 2001). Going back several decades, he discovered a myriad of reasons why we have stopped seeking civic engagement—why we have become increasingly disconnected from one another. Television, women entering the workforce, mobility, immigration, technology, and fear of strangers were just a few of the factors that appeared in his hypothesis. His bottom line was that our sense of community has collapsed and social reforms will not revive it unless people resolve to become reconnected with their friends and neighbors.

About the same time Putnam was doing his fact-finding, futurist and marketing consultant Faith Popcorn coined a term for just how removed from significant social contact so many in our culture were becoming. She called it cocooning, a reference to the way people could easily spin themselves into a sense of seclusion or safety with gated communities, homes with security systems, luxury automobiles with alarms (i.e., mobile cocoons), and access-restricted offices and factories. Popcorn pointed out that the capability of reducing uninvited interaction or the possibility of invasion was within reach of most in the middle class—and already a possession of the upper class.

More than a decade later, the social butterflies have not emerged en masse: cocooning is still with us. In fact, it has become even more prevalent, partly because uncertain economic conditions tend to drive us inward rather than outward. Millions now work first or second jobs from home, and researchers say that number will increase in the days to come.

Furthermore, so much of what used to be done in the marketplace, shoulder to shoulder with friends and neighbors, can now be done in the security and solitude of our cocoons. Stand in line at the bank? No need when there's online banking. Visit the library? Why bother when you can download the latest books right to your favorite handheld device? Push a steel cart through the grocery store? Not when you can fill your online cart with simple clicks and have it all brought to your door. Certainly not everyone is at this point, but it's easily doable and done more and more all the time.

Additionally, you can now earn a bachelor's degree at your desk in the den, go for a run on your treadmill in the basement, play tennis in front of your 50-inch plasma in the family room, and listen to religious services via a podcast anywhere in the house.

This is why so many people these days don't even know who many of their neighbors are, let alone know them on a deeper level.

When we do connect socially, we do it carefully, with people whose profiles are deemed to be compatible with our own. Popcorn called it clanning, defined as belonging to generally smaller, well-defined groups that share common causes or ideals. That's because when we find people like us, the interaction has a way of validating our own belief system. After all, engaging with different beliefs can be confrontational, and nobody wants to deal with that these days—at least not in person. (Although, somebody else's confrontation on network news or a reality show is tolerable because we can always turn it off when we get uncomfortable.)

If you're reading Invisible Neighbors in a church small group, it's likely a clan, made up of people who embrace the same creed and have the same convictions. You might even live in the same part of town, be about the same age, and have a number of the same interests. That's not unusual because it's how most of us like to do things, or at least have gotten used to doing things.

Interestingly, clanning and cocooning have now united in social networking. We can select and sort our friends, and then communicate when it's convenient from a place of comfort or safety using short sentences or an assortment of symbols. (We can even "unfriend" folks when they frustrate us, and never have to tell them to their face.) Most of the time in social networking we end up being twaddle brokers more often than communication starters. We pass along pictures or videos from friends of friends and links that are liked by people we haven't actually seen in months.

So many of us are up to our earbuds in electronic chitchat with those in our clan that we are missing valuable opportunities for eye-to-eye and heart-to-heart communication with those around us—with neighbors we know, neighbors we don't know, and neighbors we don't even know we have.

In all likelihood, down the road from you is an elderly, ailing couple without kids. Their doorbell rings even less than their phone. Government checks cover the utilities bill and little else. Typical household chores have become hard labor, but asking for assistance—from agencies or people—is not in their nature.

Almost certainly, up the street from you are two deeply discouraged newlyweds who haven't had the heart to tell their distant relatives that the bank just started foreclosure. She is showing signs that their family will increase in a few short months. He is showing no one his shame and anger with their situation.

And probably, somewhere closer than you think, a rusty van is parked in a blind alley. The woman and child inside just finished a dinner of crackers and peanut butter, washed down with water. In a little while they will roll out the carpet remnant they use for a mattress. They'll cover themselves with a thin blanket and say a prayer that their vehicle will not draw the attention of vandals or police during the night. Tomorrow they will check out the local rescue mission to see if they can get something hot to eat, and possibly a heavier blanket.

And just maybe they will make a face-to-face connection with someone who isn't wrapped up in a cocoon or too preoccupied with a clan—someone who can see their deep hurt and give them new hope.

## CONNECT

Rate your own cocooning on a scale of 1 to 10, with 1 being totally free and 10 being totally wrapped up. Are you interested in moving up or down on the scale, or content to be where you are?

How much of our cocooning and even clanning can be traced to busyness? If we read Psalm 39:4-7 each morning, would it make us change anything about the way we lived each day?

In what ways is your church encouraging or discouraging clanning? Is there a positive side of clanning that hasn't been discussed?

Social networking aside, how many new friends have you made in your local area during the last two months? How diverse are your friendships in terms of race, age, and religion?

What are five things you could cut out of your life to allow more time for those around you? What would happen if you actually did this?

## GO DEEPER

Watch/listen to Denise Hildreth Jones talk about the "Distraction of Busyness" and discuss it as a group. Go to http://www.invisibleneighbors.org/pages/video

# Part Three: The Samaritan Saga

Jesus was quite the storyteller. It was in His blood. All throughout their history, the Hebrews communicated their heritage with narratives. Their rabbis were known for their parables, and Jesus, judging partly by the crowds He drew, was a master narrator.

One day an expert in Jewish law asked Jesus how the word neighbor should be interpreted. To rise to the level of legal authority—with hundreds of detailed laws to study—was a significant achievement. Still, the meaning of this one word troubled the man. The two were talking about it in the context of the commandment to love your neighbor as yourself.

The Jews generally interpreted neighbor to mean other Jews—people of the same heritage, culture, beliefs, and lifestyle. The expert was hoping Jesus would verify the accepted understanding and thereby validate his probable practice.

No sooner did the question leave the lawyer's lips than Jesus launched into story. What He told has been retold countless times down through the centuries as the saga of The Good Samaritan. The Bible covers it in Luke 10:25-37. Take some time and read it right now.

The basic Sunday school lesson usually taught in conjunction with this tale is to show kindness to people, even when others do not. However, Jesus' stories always contain multiple layers of truth. If we take the time to consider the setting and examine His words, deeper meanings invariably emerge.

The 17-mile stretch between Jerusalem and Jericho was a constant crime scene—so much so that it was commonly called the "Way of Blood." Outlaws loved it; travelers loathed it. The evildoers would sometimes orchestrate the aftermath of a mugging on the side of the highway: One of their own would fain injury, and when a concerned passerby would come to his aid, he would be jumped, beaten, robbed, and left for dead himself.

It could have been this knowledge that prompted the priest to cut across the road when he saw his injured fellow Jew. Even though priests were the religious leaders and exemplified how to follow the law, maybe this man felt that such an uncertain scene wasn't worth risking his own safety. Moreover, priests were always busy about God's work. This one was possibly returning from his two-week rotation at the temple in Jerusalem, anxious to get back to everything that had been left unattended at home in his absence. Most certainly, somebody else would soon follow and take care of this unfortunate, inconvenient matter.

The person soon to follow was the Levite. Although priests and Levites were both from the same lineage, Levites had less eminence. This likely afforded them more flexibility with their schedules. But that didn't seem to make a difference to this guy. He followed in the way of his icon, the priest.

But the real rub in this parable for every Jew who heard it was having a Samaritan ride in to the rescue. The Jews considered the Samaritans to be mongrels with messed-up theology. The hatred was substantial and mutual. The irony that isn't mentioned in the story is that the man the Samaritan helped would have probably spit in his face had he been in better condition.

In the end, the legal expert did not get the interpretation of neighbor for which he was hoping. As usual, Jesus' words changed everything. The lawyer was being told that he now needed to reach outside his comfort zone if he wanted to please God.

To the priest and the Levite, the person in need was essentially invisible. They sensed an awkward situation but didn't see the heart of the matter. They looked away like many important and busy people of faith still do today. And when you look away enough times, you train yourself to overlook those right in front of you.

To truly love a neighbor—even the ones you never before realized you had—requires a focus not on your own desires, your busy schedule, or need for security, but instead on hurting people and their problems.

Dr. Martin Luther King, Jr. noted that in the story of the Good Samaritan, the first question the priest and Levite each asked was, "'If I stop to help this man, what will happen to me?' But then the Good Samaritan came by, and he reversed the question: 'If I do not stop to help this man, what will happen to him?'"

More than ever before, our cities, towns, and villages are full of neighbors in need. As we journey in their midst, we can play the part of the priest, the Levite, or the Samaritan. But be warned: If you lean toward the latter, once the invisible become visible, you will sense Jesus' call to a whole new level of engagement—a level from which all who claim Jesus as Lord can begin to transform society.

Dr. King talked about this, too, in a speech delivered decades ago in New York City. He said, "On the one hand we are called to play the Good Samaritan on life's roadside, but that will be only an initial act. One day we must come to see that the whole Jericho road must be transformed so that men and women will not be constantly beaten and robbed as they make their journey on life's highway. True compassion is more than flinging a coin to a beggar; it is not haphazard and superficial. It comes to see that an edifice which produces beggars needs restructuring."

But restructuring can't begin until the invisible become visible, and we see all of our neighbors from Jesus' point of view.

CONNECT

If the Levite in the story knew a priest was ahead of him, is it possible that he based his own response on that of his superior? What percent of Christians today do you think are more dependent on the examples of their spiritual leaders than on Scripture?

From the account in Scripture, what are all the ways that the Samaritan actually helped the Jew? How significant was spending the night in the same place with him?

Do you see some of yourself in James' and John's response to being rejected by the Samaritans in Luke 9:51-56? How about when it comes to people of other faiths in other countries?

When was the last time you really risked something to help someone in need? What did you learn, and under what circumstances would you do it again?

Could it be that loving your neighbor as yourself is actually the proof that you indeed love the Lord your God? What does loving with all your strength look like?

GO DEEPER

Watch the disturbing video of Angel Torres being struck by a car on a busy Hartford, Connecticut, street. Discuss why so many drivers and pedestrians did not stop to help, and what each person in the group would have done had he or she been on the scene. Go to:

http://www.invisibleneighbors.org/pages/video

# SESSION ONE NOTES

# GROUP PRAYER & PRAISE SHEET

Briefly share your prayer requests as a group, recording the requests below. Remember to record any answers to prayer below.

| PERSON | PRAYER REQUEST | PRAISE RESPONSE |
|--------|----------------|-----------------|
|        |                |                 |
|        |                |                 |
|        |                |                 |
|        |                |                 |
|        |                |                 |
|        |                |                 |
|        |                |                 |
|        |                |                 |
|        |                |                 |
|        |                |                 |
|        |                |                 |
|        |                |                 |
|        |                |                 |
|        |                |                 |
|        |                |                 |
|        |                |                 |

Engage: Watch Session Two on video

Exactly how many invisible neighbors are scattered across the United States and Canada is hard to determine, The numbers are somewhat nebulous, primarily because definitions and rules for counting impoverished people keep changing—sometimes to shield politicians. Another reason that the numbers are vague is that the definition of poor is subject to change, particularly in times of economic instability. What we do know is that the buzz about homelessness and hunger is sending heavy vibrations into all sectors of our societies in North America these days.

Government-commissioned statisticians are constantly busy measuring movement above or below established baselines. Pundits use the analyses—which more often than not are hypotheses—to help qualify various agencies for funding or prove somebody's unworthiness to be reelected. Who you listen to generally determines what numbers you get. That's because in North America, we have a way of repeatedly proving the popular adage: "Torture the data long enough and it will confess to anything."

But don't be fooled; not everybody who is homeless is sleeping beside a dumpster or in a doorway. The hidden homeless are legion. They are those who move from relative to relative or squat for the winter in somebody's summer cottage (unbeknownst to the owners) or scrape together enough coinage to extend their stay another night in a cheap motel.

Whether they are conspicuous or concealed, the plight of homeless people is a reoccurring agenda item for town and city council meetings coast to coast. For this reason there is a high demand for accurate, unbiased data. Government agencies such as the Department of Housing and Urban Development (HUD) and the Substance Abuse and Mental Health Services Administration (SAMHSA), plus private organizations including the National Law Center on Homelessness and Poverty and the National Alliance to End Homelessness, are overflowing with statistics about how many people in the United States they believe are without permanent shelter. At the time of this publication, their numbers range from about 650,000 on a given day (HUD) to approximately 850,000 in a given week (SAMHSA), and 3.5 million over the course of a year.

However, some homelessness awareness advocates accuse HUD of grossly understating the problem because of its more restrictive definition of homelessness. For example, HUD does not count the people in permanent supportive housing programs who came from the street, and only counts some of the people in rapid re-housing programs. In many of these cases, we are talking about people with no income and inadequate domestic skill having merely a government-given roof over their heads. In essence, the government has replaced their cardboard boxes with concrete boxes. Whether they are really no longer homeless or simply homeless with a solid address is the source of great debate. Additionally, HUD does not consider individuals or families homeless if they are living doubled up with other families. Indeed, the numbers can be confusing.

In Canada, official estimates of people currently homeless are in the 150,000 range, but focused studies, such as one from the Calgary-based Sheldon Chumir Foundation for Ethics in Leadership, argue that the number is double that. Canada, like the United States, also struggles with finding an accepted definition of homelessness.

Depending on how you define the term homeless, you could probably make a case for there being upward of a million people in the United States and Canada fitting into that category every night. To put that into perspective, that is the number of people it would take to fill every seat in every National Hockey League arena in North America—twice!

Regardless of the debate over definition, everyone seems to be in agreement that children and families—single mothers with children, single fathers with children, and intact families—are the fastest growing segments of the population to be homeless. While the problem used to be characterized by those Great Depression-era photos of suited men standing in line outside of a mission, looking for "three hots and a cot," it's now a full-blown family affair.

The lack of affordable housing is commonly cited as the biggest cause of family homelessness today. The generally accepted guideline is that housing costs, including taxes and utilities, should be no more than 30 percent of a household's gross income. If it is greater than 30 percent, in theory, the residents can't afford to be living there.

Most people start out living in places they can afford (although loose lending practices in the last decade make that debatable), but over time, an influx of wealthier, more educated residents might increase property values above what long-time tenants can pay. Unfortunately, moving out can mean moving away from their place of employment and support network. The other side of the sword is felt by those whose income goes down because of pay cuts, or goes away altogether because of layoffs. This even affects those living in economically stable communities. When public assistance and patience run out, moving on may be the only option.

Mental illness and substance abuse top the long list of reasons for homelessness of single people. Back in the 1960s, there was a movement to do away with mental asylums—which were generally overcrowded, unhealthy, and fostered abuse of patients—in favor of more humane and less expensive community-based treatment programs. Aided by the introduction of new and improved psychotropic drugs, the plan was touted to be the modern solution for treating those with mental disorders and developmental disabilities. While bringing an end to asylum mayhem was a decent thing to do, this alternative plan didn't work as well as predicted; far too many people fell through the cracks and ended up on the streets. That's still the case. Estimates of how many homeless people have some kind of mental illness range between 20 and 45 percent. Whatever the number, very few are receiving treatment of any kind.

Debaters can go 'round and 'round about whether some people are homeless because they are addicts or if they are addicts because they are homeless. Regardless of where you land, the truth is that a high number of homeless people, possibly as many as half, are on some level dependent on alcohol or drugs or both. Studies by the U.S. Department of Veterans Affairs found that 70 percent of homeless veterans were addicts.

A separate chapter could be written just on the issue of hunger. Suffice it to say, tens of millions of North Americans go hungry every day or are considered to be food insecure, meaning they are at risk of not having enough to eat. In fact, at the time of this publication, the U.S. Department of Agriculture claimed that 50.2 million people—including 17.2 million children—lived in food insecure households. These are people who have to choose between food and other basic necessities, such as rent, utilities, and medical care.

Severe hunger in the United States and Canada is hard to imagine when you're looking through the sneeze guard at an all-you-can-eat buffet, but recent reports show that hunger is actually increasing at an alarming rate. Of course this continent's issues are nothing like those of Africa and Asia, but when you haven't swallowed anything nutritious in three days, your stomach doesn't care if you're in India or Indiana. The only difference is that in Indiana, there are plenty of people around who can quickly solve the problem—if those in need are not invisible.

If you want somebody else's latest numbers, there is no shortage of websites providing statistics on hunger, homelessness, abuse, and addiction. But the problem with numbers is that they don't have eyes and ears and mouths. Those who claim Jesus as Lord should be generally aware of the statistics, but fully attentive to the individuals. It is the individual who is created in God's image, whom Jesus died to redeem, and who is desperately longing to be seen.

## CONNECT

Has anyone in your group ever been homeless? If so, what are some of the emotions that went along with the experience?

What is the rate of unemployment in your state or province, or in your local area? What is your church doing, or what else could it be doing, to assist those affected?

What do you think Jesus would say about the prevalence of all-you-can-eat buffets in a land where millions are suffering from hunger or are food insecure? How would He describe such places to His disciples?

What do you think should be done with all of the homeless people who are dealing with a mental illness? Why do you think churches rarely talk about this problem?

What does Matthew 10:29 imply about the value of a sparrow to God? How do you explain homelessness in light of this verse?

## GO DEEPER

Watch/listen to Dolce Wang's video on hunger in America. Ask how many in the group know people who are food insecure and what the group members are doing about it. Ask if any have been in that position themselves, and if so, have them describe the experience. Go to http://www.youtube.com/watch?v=RI53y2jOs3g.

ALTERNATE: Watch/listen to the USA Today video on "The New Homeless." Have each member of the group talk about what they think it would be like to live in such a community. Discuss the neighbors' opposition to the temporary community being located nearby. Go to http://www.invisibleneighbors.org/pages/video

# Part Two: This is my story

Shankar Vedantam, author of The Hidden Brain (Random House, 2010), theorizes that the human mind is not good at grasping the implications of mass suffering. He writes, "We don't feel 20 times sadder when we hear that 20 people have died in a disaster than when we hear that one person has died, even though the magnitude of the tragedy is 20 times as large."

It's hard to argue with Vedantam's hypothesis. The human mind does, in fact, have a hard time amplifying agony and grief. Perhaps God made us that way to protect us from massive emotional overload.

International child-sponsorship organizations understand this. That's why they do not show the hundreds of children in a poverty-stricken village who need food and medical attention. They show just one. They tell you her name and do a close-up on her face that's aching for a smile. The human mind engages much better with one than it does with a multitude.

In the same way, when we start seeing invisible neighbors, we can look too broadly and get distracted by the fact that they are so significant in number. The problem then grows so sizable that our feelings surrounding it move from being immediate and visceral to being distant and surreal. But when we deal with people one at a time, we perceive real-life issues rather than a social epidemic.

So let's turn our attention away from the masses and meet two authentic invisible neighbors. They have had poignant life journeys. Their stories are true, but their names have been changed for obvious reasons.

### Darby's Story

Darby Madison was a lean blond from the Gulf Coast. An only child, she grew up fast and married quickly after her parents passed prematurely.

By day, her young husband installed car stereos in a franchised shop. By night, he did the same, but for half the price in a friend's garage. Despite the moonlighting money, his longtime crack habit kept them poor. She only touched the stuff a few times, but equally suffered its consequences.

In their first five years together he was fired four times. Each release resulted in an arduous move. By the time they landed in Colorado, the couple had two children.

Darby never considered her marriage to be in trouble. It seemed woefully normal, the same as all the marriages she had known as a kid: plenty of fights, occasional minor physical abuse, and regular periods of estrangement. But one summer night, after an argument about there being no food in the house, her husband shoved her face-first into the side of the refrigerator. He pinned her there with his shoulder, and then grabbed her tightly by the hair and twisted her head. With his mouth inches from her ear, his loud, expletive-laced rant crushed her spirit: She was worthless; he was leaving. He then kicked open the front door and disappeared beyond the stream of the streetlight.

After several months of not knowing her husband's whereabouts, the stress of waiting for word while working two part-time jobs and caring for the kids got to be more than Darby could bear alone. She phoned a single aunt three states away. With tears flowing, Darby made arrangements to sublet a bedroom from her. She used most of her available money for the move.

The adult conversation was a welcome change, but life was still tough because jobs were harder to come by in this new location. All she could find was 25 hours a week behind the counter at a convenience store. And then life got tougher: The aunt received notice that their apartment complex was being taken over by order of eminent domain. All residents had 30 days to vacate.

For two weeks, they looked for an affordable place to rent, but gentrification was altering the area's economics. Midway through the third week, a cousin in Calgary reluctantly agreed to take in the aunt, but made it abundantly clear that he didn't have room for Darby and the kids. The fourth week was spent sorting clothes and selling belongings. She and the kids stayed for a while at the Y, and then their money ran out.

Never religious, Darby determined it was time to seek help from the spiritual community. She went to a church that reminded her a lot of one near her childhood home. The pastor was friendly enough, but when Darby asked if the church had some place she and the kids could stay until she got back on her feet, he replied, "We're not really set up to do that kind of thing. But you might try County Social Services."

Someone told Darby that if she went to County Social Services they would take her kids. She instantly ruled out that option.

Today, Darby's children are ages seven and five. The three of them are still together in Boston where Darby bunks in with a man twice her age. She abhors him for what he requires of her in return for shelter, but it's better than the street. He makes Darby buy her own food. She earns the money by hustling people for historic tours in the city's North End. It's a scant, unpredictable wage, but usually enough for a few groceries to sustain her and the kids.

She longs for a place of her own, a decent job, and a good school for the children. But her husband's words still resound in her head as if they were delivered just yesterday. And she now has come to believe she really is worthless. Sadly, Darby has no loving neighbors to convince her otherwise.

## Clayton's Story

Clayton Talley was raised in the Rust Belt. Even as a kid he knew there was no future for him in his formidable city. With high school graduation just months away, he decided it would be just as easy to survive in Saigon as it would in the hood, so he walked the stage and straight away traded in his cap and gown for a helmet and fatigues. Eighteen weeks later, the U.S. Army had him wading in rice paddies.

Despite occasionally being shot at, Clayton's first tour of duty in Vietnam turned out to be the best years of his life. With some extra training, the Army qualified him as a truck mechanic and stationed him at a high-security base. He made several good friends in his unit, and every weekend pass was a ticket to international adventure.

Clayton re-upped when it came time, but his second tour was nothing like the first. He was reassigned. Fighting intensified. Every day he lived somewhere between total confusion and sheer panic. On a move north, his convoy ran into intense shelling and took heavy casualties. While Clayton was dragging a buddy out from under a burning chassis, a shell exploded nearby, implanting shrapnel deeply into his left leg, severing tendons and breaking bones. He did the hospital circuit in Vietnam, Germany, and the States, and served out his stint at a base on the West Coast. He left the Army with a couple of medals and a noticeable limp.

With his Uncle Sam no longer around, Clayton looked for a job as a mechanic, but his impairment, his race, and anti-Vietnam War sentiment were all working against him. Perspective employers would say, "Boy, you were in the military; you were only trained to kill people. Go get certified for real, then come back and see us."

Los Angeles was a big city, but janitorial and sanitation jobs were about all he could find for the next few years. On weeknights and weekends he would meet up with other vets in a park. They would swap war stories and commiserate about their assorted injuries and misfortunes. It didn't help his situation, but it felt good to have people with whom he could share his despair.

Clayton eventually moved further east and landed a job at a feedlot, but the high-plains cold got to him—especially bothering his bad leg. Someone suggested that rye whiskey could make him impervious to harsh temperatures and bitter winds. It didn't work, but he and Jim Beam became pretty good friends anyway. Sometimes he and Jim would skip work entirely and spend the day together. Eventually, every morning started with a stern warning from his annoying boss. Clayton decided it was time to move on before somebody got hurt.

Each decade to follow found him a little further east, doing menial labor for meager pay—but somehow there was always enough to buy booze. The alcohol kept him buzzed and poor.

A barroom brawl in Nashville landed him in the slammer for one whole weekend. During the booking, he heard the police throw around the words bum and drunk. Even in his stupor, it registered that they were talking about him. The next 48 hours were spent staring at the ceiling of a cell and wondering how he got where he was and what would be his destiny. For the first time, he saw himself as others did, and it was a dismal portrait.

Four years ago, Clayton moved back to Detroit. His old neighborhood was nothing like he remembered. In fact, it looked more like some of the bombed-out places he used to come across in Vietnam. Everybody he knew was long gone.

These days he sleeps in a shed behind an auto body shop. The owner doesn't bother him. In fact, he occasionally has Clayton sweep up around the place in exchange for fresh coffee and a few dollars. Clayton often thinks of the irony of escaping his city, only to end up back there as a prisoner of poverty and his poor choices. He wonders if there will ever be another opportunity for him. Now on the high side of 60, he seriously doubts it. Furthermore, he has no concerned neighbors to inspire him, even if something were to come his way.

## CONNECT

What emotions did you experience as you read Darby's story? If you could jump into her life at any point in the past to help her, when would it be and what would you do?

What goes through your mind when you remember that single women with young children are the fastest growing segment of the population to be homeless? What do you believe will be the long-term effects on people who were homeless as children?

What upsets you about Clayton's story? With whom should you be upset?

Have you ever encountered anybody on the street who could be Clayton? If you saw that person tomorrow, what would you say to him, now that you've read Clayton's story?

With Jesus being fully man and fully God, do you think he was able to amplify agony and grief in a way we cannot? If so, how would that have made His final hour on the cross if He was not dying for the singular "sins of the world" but for the infinitely compounded sins of every individual who ever lived?

## GO DEEPER

Break up into groups of two or three and spend a morning or afternoon in a public park in a larger city. Sit down beside some of the people you encounter and ask them to tell you their stories. Don't be afraid to ask questions. When you get back together as a larger group, talk about what you learned. Note: You may want to take a snack, coffee, or lunch into the park and share it with those you engage.

# Part Three: The Next Ten Years

What a tremendous relief it is to wake up from a nightmare and discover that what you have just dreamt is not true. It's like a soothing salve for the psyche.

In the same way, wouldn't it be wonderful if we got up next Monday morning and discovered that hunger, homelessness, abuse, and addiction had somehow disappeared, or were decreasing so rapidly that they were predicted to be gone altogether in ten years? There would be unprecedented rejoicing in the streets. Right?

Probably not. While we might like the idea of ending hunger, homelessness, abuse, and addiction, putting a stop to these social ills would require most of society to abruptly let go of selfish human values and instead embrace unselfish godly values. And most of us—Christ-followers included—do not seem all that interested in straying too far from the values we have chosen and come to love. Churches have preached for centuries that the world must be forsaken if Christ's kingdom is to be realized, but it seems we're now further than ever from "his kingdom come."

How does the human value system operate? Let's say we took 100 people, all in good health and of normal intelligence, and put them on a large deserted island to live out their lives. Within a short period of time, about 20 people would work their way to the top, because their standout ideas and hard work would result in the harvesting of more resources, which would allow for greater possessions, and ultimately more influence over the others.

In the same amount of time, another 20 or so people would become disillusioned and upset with the system and its structures, and rebel against the established codes and mores. Ultimately, their survival and everyone else's contentment would be contingent on the whole population providing for them. Another 10, plus or minus a few, would over time become chronically ill or severely injured and need help from the able-bodied on the island.

The other approximately 50 people would be spread out somewhere between the top and the bottom, envying the former and resenting the later. It's a predictable sociological eventuality.

Regardless of where one starts on the vertical continuum, the human value system constantly impels people to reach the top—even in Christian circles—for a sense of achievement and notoriety, and the rewards that come with those things. The human value system does encourage dabbling at the bottom, but generally in order to present a pretense of altruism. Being at the top is really the end goal. Occasionally you'll see on car bumpers and T-shirts the ignoble summary slogan of this system: "He who dies with the most toys wins."

But God's value system flips everything on its head. It drives you the opposite direction. Fully following God's value system is a race to the bottom, to lift up those who are there. That's because in God's value system, success is not measured by how much we get but by how much we give. It's not about how many we can manipulate but how many we can serve.

For those who agree with this and want to truly follow God's way—the way that Jesus taught—there's good news: Your opportunities during the next ten years will be disturbingly abundant.

Many of the people who are homeless today had no idea six months ago that they would be in such dire straits. Bad investments and risky loans have consumed the savings and destroyed the equity of more people than anyone cares to count. Just as many are one sharp drop in the Dow or one interest-rate hike away from the same fate. The politicians in power—regardless of party—would like us to think that the picture is brighter now that they're in charge, but learned economists are right behind them with their reality pallets to dab the painting with darker colors.

Across the continent, most of the 10-year plans to end homelessness are now in their second decade and show no signs that they won't go into their third. Not long before this publication, Dr. J. David Hulchanski, with the faculty of social work at the University of Toronto, gave an address on Canada's past, present, and future homeless. He stated, "Sadly, the future of homelessness in Canada...looks very bright." He suggested that while there were ways to curtail it, "Homelessness, as well as other manifestations of poverty, can become much worse as our support systems are further weakened and our public priorities remain elsewhere." The next ten years are, of course, hard to accurately predict, but all of the elements are certainly in place to keep homelessness high for the foreseeable future.

As the economy continues to struggle, the implications of immigration complicate the homeless crisis. Immigration, legal and illegal, is the largest factor contributing to population growth in the United States and Canada. The total foreign-born population in the United States alone is now in the 40 million range. The U.S Census Bureau projected that if policies remain as they are, the U.S. population will double this century.

A large number of immigrants fall below the poverty line. They currently make up 11 percent of the U.S. population—and 20 percent of the poor. A USA Today study from a few years ago showed that about one-third of adult immigrants have not completed high school, which tends to be a common denominator in predicting poverty and chronic homelessness. Regardless of where you weigh in on the issue, recent immigrants are many of our invisible neighbors, and in the next ten years will represent amazing opportunities for those interested in displaying God's value system.

And then there is the issue of the elderly. We've been warned for years that many retiring Baby Boomers—those born between 1946 and 1964, 70-plus million strong—will outlive their money. Some estimates say that will be true of about half. Many of these seniors will be cared for by their children and grandchildren, but what about the rest? When we think of helping the poor we usually don't think of 70- and 80-year-olds. If we are future-minded, we will need to start thinking in that direction. While nobody really knows how this scenario surrounding seniors will unfold during the next ten years, it will surely add another layer of complexity to the issue of invisible neighbors.

## CONNECT

In what ways do you find yourself getting caught up in the human value system? What would be the ramifications of changing at this point in your life?

In Matthew 19:20-22, did Jesus actually mean that the young man should sell everything he had and give it to the poor? Is that same advice applicable to all Christ-followers or just those who are caught up in their wealth?

What do you think could be the best-case scenario and the worst-case scenario regarding homelessness during the next ten years? How is the church gearing up to respond in case the latter comes to pass?

What position should Christ-followers take on undocumented immigrants and their access to services in the country where they are living? If a known undocumented immigrant came to you in need, would you assist him or her or contact the authorities?

Do you think aging Baby Boomers will produce a generation of elderly poor, or do you see a solution on the horizon? Could the outliving of money affect anybody close to you, and if so, what plans have you discussed with them?

## GO DEEPER

Watch/listen to Dr. Will Varner address the issue of how Christians should treat immigrants. Talk about his perspective and see how many in your group agree with him. What other Scripture-supported perspectives surface in your group? Go to http://www.invisibleneighbors.org/pages/video

ALTERNATE: Watch John Piper answer an impromptu question about how a pastor should respond to a congregation of illegal immigrants. Talk about his answer and see how many in your group agree with him. What other Scripture-supported answers surface in your group? http://www.invisibleneighbors.org/pages/video

# SESSION TWO NOTES

_____

_____

_____

_____

_____

_____

_____

_____

_____

_____

_____

_____

_____

_____

_____

# GROUP PRAYER & PRAISE SHEET

Briefly share your prayer requests as a group, recording the requests below. Remember to record any answers to prayer below.

| PERSON | PRAYER REQUEST | PRAISE RESPONSE |
|--------|----------------|-----------------|
|        |                |                 |
|        |                |                 |
|        |                |                 |
|        |                |                 |
|        |                |                 |
|        |                |                 |
|        |                |                 |
|        |                |                 |
|        |                |                 |
|        |                |                 |
|        |                |                 |
|        |                |                 |
|        |                |                 |
|        |                |                 |
|        |                |                 |
|        |                |                 |
|        |                |                 |

Engage: Watch Session Three on video

# THE QUESTION OF RESPONSIBILITY

## PART ONE: THE GOVERNMENT'S BURDEN?

"Never discuss religion and politics in polite company" is an axiom so old that nobody remembers who said it first. Unfortuntaely, there's no getting around it; both have to be discussed if we want to understand and deal with the problems of hunger, homelessness, abuse, and addiction in our society. To try to do otherwise is like trying to explain water without talking about hydrogen or oxygen.

If you grew up following the fall of the Berlin Wall, there's no question in your mind: Government is duty-bound to assist the poor. It's assumed to be an unassailable civic responsibility of the powers-that-be. And if you grew up just after the Berlin Wall was built, you've become so accustomed to government telling you that it needs to handle issues of the desperate and dispossessed that you go along with it whether you agree in theory or not.

But it wasn't always that way. When North America was first settled, the family unit, not the government, was the safety net to catch individuals who, for whatever reason, had lost their footing in life. Having a plethora of children ensured compassionate care, regardless of condition, from cradle to grave. The family would also come together to help those wandering in the woods get back on the right road.

With the Industrial Revolution and mass migration to urban areas, the average number of children per family began to decline. In the United States, from 1800 and 1900, it went from seven children per family to three and a half. Today it is a finite fraction over two per family. In Canada, it is about half that.

Not only are families now smaller, but they also live farther apart. In agrarian societies, each child got a piece of the farm and lived just across the corn from each other and "the folks." As we moved from an agrarian society to a manufacturing society and then to an information-technology society, families scattered far and wide—and in many cases, lost some of the emotional attachment, too. Today, if it weren't for Skype, some families wouldn't see each other for months or years at a time. It's easy to see that there are huge holes in the family-unit safety net.

For a period of time, towns and villages did an admirable job of coming alongside family units within their jurisdictions and helping to care for those in need; think of TV's Mayberry model—still in syndication in some places!—with Andy and Aunt Bea looking out for family, friends, and strangers. But as social capital and community connectivity continued to erode, our burgs and hamlets began to lose track and interest in those in their midst who were in want.

So government has increasingly become the fallback solution. After all, no developed country wants its citizens to lack life's essentials and suffer sustained hardships—although a spin of the globe might make you think differently. Today we have government programs to ensure that those on the lowest rungs of the economic ladder receive food, clothing, housing, education, equal opportunity, health care, old-age income, and more. Some people go to Washington and Ottawa and make careers out of producing, revising, massaging, debating, repealing, and explaining who gets what and who gets to pay for it.

Political parties are part of the culture on both sides of the 49th parallel. The major political parties have always been—and are even more so today—like volatile stars, always in a state of flux, spewing off gases and particles to form smaller bodies that make orbiting a collision waiting to happen. Based on upbringing, church affiliation, age, peer influence, personal experience, or any combination of these, people generally feel an affinity for one particular political party.

Specific political party nomenclatures aside, there are basically two competing ideologies that drive North American politics today: liberalism and conservatism. Here is essentially how they differ (borrowing definitions directly from studentnewsdaily. com).

Liberals believe in government action to achieve equal opportunity and equality for all. They say it is the government's duty to alleviate social ills and protect civil liberties and individual and human rights. Liberals believe the role of the government should be to guarantee that no one faces hardships. Liberal policies generally emphasize the need for the government to solve problems.

No well-balanced individual would argue that equal opportunity, equality, the alleviation of social ill, civil liberties, and human rights are immoral concepts. The stiff disagreements come over determining what actuality constitutes civil liberties and human rights, and how to achieve them.

On the other side of the political spectrum, conservatives believe in personal responsibility, limited government, free markets, individual liberty, traditional values, and a strong national defense. Conservatives believe the role of government should be to provide people the freedom necessary to pursue their own goals. Conservative policies generally emphasize empowerment of the individual to solve problems.

Again, who can argue that these things are not foundational in most democracies? But deciding where one person's pursuit of a goal starts to infringe on another person's human rights produces tumult and tense debate.

The benevolence of liberalism has a flip side that looks a lot like addiction, creating a populace of dependants who can't say no to the free elixir for life's problems. What starts out as temporary reinforcement is seen over time as a permanent entitlement. To take it back or even cut it back is to risk near revolution. No country promising so much to so many can sustain such a system indefinitely.

But conservatism as we know it has not produced an alternative answer. Despite the emphasis on personal empowerment to solve society's problems, there is no groundswell of support within the rank and file for social justice. In other words, conservative ideology is all about having the freedom from government to creatively produce independent programs and services to serve the good of all mankind. Unfortunately, a noticeable, widespread consuming passion to help the less fortunate does not exist. For all of its laudable ideals, conservatism has shown itself to be rather selfish.

In the context of invisible neighbors, conservatives see liberals as overextended socialists; liberals see conservatives as overcritical and selfish. Both sides are correct to some degree.

Two recent U.S. presidents—one conservative and one liberal—recognized that government and independent groups need to work together to handle the problems facing hungry, homeless, abused, and addicted people. The first president started the White House Office of Faith-based and Community Initiatives. The second president kept it going as the White House Office of Faith-based and Neighborhood Partnerships.

These attempts at greater public-private collaboration are commendable, but the results are mixed. Numerous faith-based groups have formed productive partnerships with the government to serve the poor, while others are more comfortable carrying out their faith-based mission of serving the poor apart from government involvement. An intricately woven web of laws makes working with the government a sticky situation for some faith groups. For others, it's something to avoid entirely. Regardless, the size of the problems facing our communities will require ongoing teamwork and the involvement of all willing partners—government, religious groups, and community-based organizations, nonprofit, and for-profit.

## CONNECT

Does your own family have a strong network of support in place for times of crisis? How is it manifested and maintained?

Outside of family, what people you know—particularly those going through economic hard times—leaning on for their support? What are the potential breakdowns in their plans?

If Jesus physically lived in North America today, when it came to matters of the poor, would He side more often with the liberals or the conservatives? Can you defend you answer from Scripture?

If our political authorities behave in ways with which we disagree, or appropriate public funds for programs we oppose, what does Romans 13:1-7 suggest we do or not do? How does this Scripture passage apply to us in modern, pluralistic democracies?

Do you think having the government and churches—as well as other faith-based organizations—working together on matters of social concern is a good or bad idea? What will be the end result if the government and faith-based organizations never work together or become close partners?

GO DEEPER

Go to http://www.invisibleneighbors.org/pages/video and watch U.S. President Barak Obama and Joshua DuBois talk about the office of Faith-Based and Neighborhood Partnerships, and then discuss what's happening in your own city or county, and what else could be done.

ALTERNATE: As a group, watch the clip from whatyououghttoknow.com at http://www.invisibleneighbors.org/pages/video about the difference between liberals and conservatives, and discuss the commentator's perspectives.

## Part Two: The Church's Responsibility?

The Gospels and the Epistles could not be more clear that anyone who desires to wholly follow Jesus has a responsibility to the poor and oppressed. Also explicit in the New Testament is that the church is the divinely chosen channel to nurture and empower saints to do kingdom work. In short, the church has an enormous and enduring social obligation. Sadly, in some respects, the church has surrendered much of its charge to the government.

To say that churches are not engaged in the fight against hunger, homelessness, abuse, and addiction would be an improper portrayal of the bride of Christ. Certainly many congregations, particularly in urban areas, are aware of their invisible neighbors and are warmly welcoming them into their midst, or at least helping them find the accommodations and programs they need.

But to imply that Christ-followers are charging the front lines en masse as a disciplined army, anxious to do battle against these social woes and defend the tenets of His kingdom, is simply not true. There is certainly more talk about it than ever before, but talk does not win the war.

In searching for a reason why the church has not been fully engaged, you find that the organizing and professionalizing of Christian ministry during the last century or so is as much to blame as anything.

In the frontier days of North America, and generally on up through the time of the U.S. Civil War, individual churches, large or small, were the driving force in ministry. It was the single church that sent missionaries to Africa or China, cared for the widows and orphans in their communities, and opened soup kitchens to feed those who weren't getting enough to eat. This was at a time when Christian values were still warmly embraced in public schools, so the youth generally heard endorsements of these ministries on a daily basis.

Denominations existed, but because communications and transportation were still rudimentary, they didn't have the presence and wherewithal to oversee a lot of what was going on in their churches, especially in rural areas. As this changed with the onset of the twentieth century, denominations took more control of programs and

communications. They added their own brand to ministry by starting or expanding Bible schools and seminaries, forming mission boards, and introducing publishing houses that produced books and homogeneous curriculum.

The orchestrated maturation in many of the major denominations undoubtedly made people proud to be part of something so successful and far-reaching. At the same time, a subtle sense passed throughout the pews that individual members were not so much needed any longer for their work as they were for their worth. After all, "corporate" had the creative component pretty well in control.

Until World War II, most ministries remained denominationally driven, but that global conflict changed everything. Tens of thousands of people, mostly men, who had never ventured more than a few miles or kilometers away from their home turfs found themselves on the other side of the world, involved in carnage and destruction. Many had "foxhole conversions" and epiphanies that reshaped their lives: "God, get me out of here in one piece and I'll follow and serve you and commit my life to correcting these terrible wrongs." Many lived up to their prayers.

The decade following World War II saw the start of thousands of independent ministries around the globe. Many of them went on to be evangelical household names: Billy Graham Evangelistic Association, World Vision, Compassion International, The Navigators, Campus Crusade for Christ, Young Life, Youth for Christ, Mission Aviation Fellowship, Greater Europe Mission, and hundreds more.

As a result, a new paradigm emerged. Celebrated ministry was no longer single-church driven or denominationally driven. Although single churches and denominations still had their unique influence, it was now by and large parachurch driven, and remained so for the next several decades. (The word parachurch essentially means alongside the church.) As a result of this proliferation of Christian organizations, the gospel message was spread far and wide and the positive energy generated in the name of Jesus lit up the field for any who wanted to follow in similar types of service.

Meanwhile, back in the pews, there was a growing sense that the "professionals" were now in charge of hands-on ministry. Anyone could join the ranks, but serious involvement customarily required a change of vocation from "secular" to "Christian" work. Of course there were always invitations to lavish prayer and financial support on the numerous ventures. Unfortunately, the average church attendees went to Sunday services and prayer meeting, and attended the annual men's retreat or woman's conference or youth camp, but couldn't help feeling pushed back even further from the front-line action.

By the early 1990s, the parachurch-driven era gave way to the megachurch-driven era. (Some well-known megachurches had been around for more than a decade by this time.) While parachurch organizations were by no means rendered irrelevant, they were no longer the contemporary driving force behind widely recognized ministry successes.

Megachurches—those with 2,000 or more in regular weekly attendance, and generally evangelical in persuasion—were not everywhere, but their influence was certainly felt far and wide. That influence spilled over to congregations that could be considered mini-megachurches—those with 500-plus members that behaved like megachurches.

The majority of megachurches were (and still are) finely tuned machines that got firm traction thanks to resources that allowed for immediate response and control of outcomes. For example, in the megachurch-driven era, there was no longer a need or desire to direct missionary candidates to parachurch sending agencies that would make them jump through two or more years of hoops before placing them abroad. Mission ventures with a megachurch, usually short-term, were spontaneous, manageable, and more in line with each megachurch's philosophy.

The megachurch-driven era gave people plenty of options for service times and wonderfully produced programs, but serious fellowship was mostly found in small groups. Moreover, hands-on ministry was handled by departments headed by capable staff who expected a higher degree of competence than had been accepted in years prior. Meanwhile, the typical person in the cushioned chair, unless he or she wanted to apply or audition, couldn't help but feel pushed back even further from prominent ministry. Desire notwithstanding, the "skilled insiders" had things covered.

To be clear, the church of Jesus Christ in North America over the last hundred years has made significant progress throughout the continent and the world. Hundreds of thousands of people have been trained, resourced, and encouraged by strong entities—denominations, parachurch organizations, and megachurches—to spread the gospel and do wonderful work in every area imaginable. But the relentless motivating and equipping of millions of others to discover and daily use their spiritual gifts for core ministry in their neighborhoods and communities has not been on the same par. Some are quick to blame it on apathy, but the church then has to wonder if it is an apathy caused by a century of disincentive.

Interestingly, the paradigm is shifting again, and the front lines are now clearly in sight.

Today, ministry is no longer single-church driven, denominationally driven, parachurch-driven, or even megachurch-driven. Today it is cause-driven, youth-led, and technology-enhanced. Those engaged are no longer about broad categories such as missions or evangelism or discipleship. They are about causes like clean water, AIDS orphans, global hunger, human trafficking, literacy, and the like. The gospel is the catalyst.

The charge to the front lines is not waiting for congregational sanctioning. It is young, energetic, diverse disciples—the primal church—racing to where the need is the greatest and getting others of like commitment to joint their efforts, all the while texting, tweeting, and posting their impressions, results, and additional needs.

Could this be the dawn of a new day of engagement for the church—particularly in the area of passionate ministry to the poor and social justice? Many believe so, especially because of the involvement of so many younger people who do not see their faith as personal, but as communal. Can it be sustained? Quite possibly, as long as the race is understood to be a marathon and not a sprint, and every person who names the name of Jesus collaborates and participates, regardless of age or technology skills.

## CONNECT

How have you seen denominations change in your lifetime? Is that a healthy or unhealthy thing for the church in general?

What are some of the parachurch organizations with which you are familiar, and how have you interacted with them? What are three things parachurches have to do to be most effective at this point in history?

How does the size of a church make a difference in what services it provides? What would have to happen for a small church—200 people or fewer—to have a major impact in its community in serving hungry, homeless, abused, and addicted people?

What are the ways that equipping, as discussed in Ephesians 4:11-13, takes place in your church? Why do you think some people believe these verses infer that the majority of work in the church is to be done by apostles, pastors, teachers, and so forth?

Where do you see cause-driven ministry taking place in the world today? Do you think this change of paradigm is a good or a bad thing for the church and its overall purpose?

## GO DEEPER

Find a church in your city or a city near you with a creative program that is helping the poor. Go and observe it, and then reconvene as a group and discuss what you saw.

ALTERNATE: Read the AGRM White Paper "The Hundred-Years War" by Dr. Bob Wenz, and discuss where you see your church in light of the article. Find it at: http://www.invisibleneighbors.org/pages/links

## Part Three: Under the Overpass

No one tells the distressing story of how some churches avoid invisible neighbors like Mike Yankoski. Mike's incredible experience of actually being an invisible neighbor is the subject of his book Under the Overpass (WaterBrook Multnomah, 2010).

While a student at a prestigious Christian college, Mike was sitting in church one Sunday listening to sermon about being a genuine Christian.  He was suddenly struck with the huge disconnect between what he said about his world and how he lived it.

Here, reprinted with permission from WaterBrook Multnomah, is just some of Mike's amazing journey.

I claimed that Christ was my stronghold, my peace, my sustenance, my joy. But I did all that from the safety of my comfortable upper-middle-class life. I never really had to put my claims to the test.

I sat there in church struggling to remember a time when I'd actually needed to lean fully on Christ rather than on my own abilities. Not much came to mind. What was Paul's statement in Philippians? "I have learned what it means to be content in all circumstances, whether with everything or with nothing." With nothing?

What resulted from this internal turmoil was Mike decision to spend more than five months on the streets with only a backpack, sleeping bag, and guitar. He and a traveling companion, Sam Purvis, explored life in six different cities as people with no means, surviving only by panhandling—playing music for spare change—and with handouts. Mike and Sam, followers of Jesus, had initially anticipated that the church would be their refuge and shelter in times of need. More often than not, this wasn't the case. In fact, some churches made it difficult for anybody to gain access.

Early on a Friday evening, just after the sun had set, Sam and I were walking from the library back down to the Portland waterfront where we had decided the Friday night crowd would offer a prime panhandling opportunity. We didn't say much as we walked until we passed a church.

"Oh, my gosh!" I exclaimed, stopping. "You've got to be kidding me."

"What?" said Sam. Then he saw where I was looking. "Oh," he murmured.

A large gray church rose up behind a wrought iron fence in front of us. The building was old and weathered. Above the mahogany double doors hung a sign in red letters. "No Trespassing. Church Business Only." A new chain and two huge padlocks secured the gate at the sidewalk.

"It would take bolt cutters and a battering ram to get into that church," I said, suddenly angry. "'Come to me all you who are weary and heavy laden'? Yeah, and what, die on my front steps?"

We turned to keep walking toward the waterfront. Sure, a church needs to protect its property, but what we had just seen seemed excessive, and sent a negative, uncaring message.

Sam was having the same thoughts. "Let's say your life is falling apart and you need help. Would you want to go there?"

"Nope," I said. "Anywhere but there. But the world is the church's business—and that's exactly who they're shutting out!"

"Correct me if I'm wrong," said Sam, "But aren't the people in a sanctuary a whole lot more important than the sanctuary itself?"

We walked past a market that sold pop, beer, wine, cigarettes, pornography. The doors were wedged open. Ragged people came and went.

It was one of the places that never close.

Of course, steeples and steps are just wood and concrete. It's the followers of Jesus who really comprise the church. It's the followers of Jesus who have compassion on the poor—sometimes.

One weekday afternoon, Sam and I walked into a D.C. sandwich shop to escape the blazing heat of the streets. It was a perfect getaway—an empty restaurant with only the hum of the air conditioner. The cowbell over the door interrupted the silence and announced our presence.

A stairway led to a second floor dining area, where we found a corner table. Shrugging off our packs and laying down the guitars, we sat down across from one another, relieved to be out of the heat even if only for a moment.

After cooling down for a bit, I walked back down the stairs to fill our water bottles. I could feel the employees behind the counter staring at me, "How's it going today guys?" I asked cheerfully. All I got in return were stony stares. My enthusiasm hadn't quite worked.

Mike went back upstairs just as several people walked up carrying lunch trays. When they caught sight of us, the lead guy hesitated. Sam and I looked down feeling ashamed that we had caused him to pause, our smiles disappearing. I sat down and pulled my bag closer, trying to give the group as much social (and breathing) space as possible.

The man regained his composure and walked over to the furthest table from us. A girl took a seat with him, while another couple sat one table away.

When another guy walked upstairs, he, too, went to the far side of the room and plunked down his tray. On it I noticed a meatball sub and a worn brown leather New Testament. Soon all five, obviously strangers to each other, were busy eating their sandwiches.

I pretended to be reading a book, and Sam did the same, but the aroma of that meatball sub was killing us.

After a couple of minutes, one of them asked the man with the Bible what translation it was.

"NIV," he answered. "What version do you read?"

"NLT," the guy answered.

"Really?" the girl from the other table chimed in. "I really like the NASB."

"I guess it's just a matter of preference," the guy in the middle said, taking another bite of his juicy meatball sub. The next ten minutes were filled with lively conversation between the five new friends. Across the room, Sam and I sat quietly, reading and reeking.

Eventually the five ate their fill and crumpled up their wrappers. Getting ready to leave, the man with the Bible told both couples he would pray for them. Both couples thanked him honestly and said the same thing in reply. As they walked past us, Sam and I looked up, trying to catch their eyes and nod a hello. But they carefully looked away. Each emptied their tray of garbage in the trashcan next to Sam and turned to walk down the stairs.

I remembered many times I had walked past a homeless man or woman sitting on the cold sidewalk, awkwardly averting my eyes and whistling to cover discomfort. I wondered if those men and women had been as frustrated with me as I now was with the people who were walking down the stairs.

As they walked out the door, the cowbell rang loudly, and reflections of sunlight flashed through the downstairs portion of the restaurant. After that, we were alone again— empty restaurant and the hum of the air conditioner.

"Did you see that?" I asked Sam, nodding to the trashcan.

"Yeah," he said with a sigh. "There's probably a whole sandwich between those five wrappers."

"Yep. You hungry"

"Sure am."

Sam looked over his shoulder at the trashcan, his sudden movement causing a couple of flies to start buzzing around the lid. Sam looked back at me and shrugged. "Here we go!" I said, rising up and lifting the lid. As I did so, several flies buzzed lazily away.

We both grabbed what looked like more recent trash and, pushing our books aside, spread it on our table. My big find was the remains of a club sandwich, only slightly mushed. I took a huge bite and started chewing, trying not to think about where the sandwich had come from or who might have had the first go at it.

Sam had scored the remains of the man's meatball sub. I asked him how his lunch tasted. "Good!" he said through a full mouth. "Yours?"

"Good! That first bite was a little shaky, but it's easier now. I'm hungry, so that always helps."

Throughout their sojourns in the six cities, Mike and Sam spent every Sunday morning at a church somewhere, longing to be welcomed into community. Sadly, the way they looked and how they smelled produced barriers that were hard for church people to overcome.

One night in Phoenix we stretched out our sleeping bags in front of a church's main doors hoping that early the next morning we would be awakened by a kindhearted churchgoer wondering if he could help us in some way. A simple, obvious plan, we thought, but it didn't work.

At about seven the next morning, while a dream of wintertime in the Rockies cooled my sweating body, a far away voice pulled me back to reality. "And before we read from Romans 8, let us pray together…"

Sam and I were still on the steps of the church and already baking in the morning sun. I rolled over to look through the sanctuary windows. A small gathering was standing while the pastor led in prayer. The early service was just getting under way inside, but for us, the voice came from a speaker just above where we slept.

"Sam," I said, nudging him awake.

"Yeah?" He sat up, shaking his head.

"Did anybody wake you up?" I said, pointing into the sanctuary.

"No way," he said. We both realized what had happened. Every person inside had gone through a side door. "Nobody woke me up. You?"

"Nope."

The pastor was ending his prayer. "Lord, teach us to look not into ourselves but unto You and unto others…" With a loud amen that came metallically through the speaker above, the congregation took its seat and he began his sermon.

Already soaked with sweat, we decided to pack up and move on. "Wow," said Sam, "I thought we were making it easy for them!"

But were we? I'm not so sure now. I think two sleeping transients on the church steps early one morning would make most people uneasy, Christian or not. The need is unexpected, out of place, and a little disturbing. Yet it is exactly here, in the difficult circumstances, that Christ's love should take risks to meet needs.  In A Ragamuffin Gospel, Brennan Manning describes what that kind of love looks like: "To evangelize a person is to say to him or her: you too are loved by God and the Lord Jesus. And not only to say it but to really think it, and relate it to them so they can sense it. But that becomes possible only by offering the person your friendship, a friendship that is real, unselfish, without condescension, full of confidence and profound esteem."

## CONNECT
Do you ever sense, like Mike did, that there is a disconnect between what you say about your faith and how you live it out from day to day? Do you think that is the case with a lot of Christians, and, if so, is there a simple solution?

Other than padlocks, how else do churches "lock out" strangers? How would you design a church to meet the pressing needs of invisible neighbors?

Does James 1:26-27, as paraphrased in The Message, describe the people who Mike and Sam encountered in the upstairs of the sandwich shop? How do Christians typically take care of widows and orphans in today's culture?

Do you agree with the inferences made by Brennan Manning that offering a person your genuine friendship is at the heart of evangelism? If so, what percentage of evangelism today would you say has friendship as its key component?

In what ways, other than in a church setting as described in James 2:1-4, can Christians show discrimination or partiality? What does it means in James 2:5 that God has chosen the poor to inherit the kingdom?

## GO DEEPER
Watch/listen to Mike Yankoski tell some of his story. Discuss the things that affected you the most about what he said. Talk about how you would have reacted to Mike and Sam if you passed them on the street. Talk about how you see your church in light of the churches Mike describes.
Go to http://www.invisibleneighbors.org/pages/video

ALTERNATE: Take a break from Invisible Neighbors and read Under the Overpass. This will be a great resource to help you better grasp the important points of Invisible Neighbors. Watch for the movie based on the book Under the Overpass; go see it as a group.

# SESSION THREE NOTES

_____

_____

_____

_____

_____

_____

_____

_____

_____

_____

_____

_____

_____

_____

# GROUP PRAYER & PRAISE SHEET

Briefly share your prayer requests as a group, recording the requests below. Remember to record any answers to prayer below.

| PERSON | PRAYER REQUEST | PRAISE RESPONSE |
|--------|----------------|-----------------|
|        |                |                 |
|        |                |                 |
|        |                |                 |
|        |                |                 |
|        |                |                 |
|        |                |                 |
|        |                |                 |
|        |                |                 |
|        |                |                 |
|        |                |                 |
|        |                |                 |
|        |                |                 |
|        |                |                 |
|        |                |                 |
|        |                |                 |
|        |                |                 |

Engage: Watch Session Four on video

# LOVE YOUR NEIGHBOR AS YOURSELF

## PART ONE: A BIBLICAL PERSPECTIVE ON THE POOR

Some future Sunday, go loiter at the door of a church—any church—and ask exiting parishioners for one standout statement the Bible makes about the poor. There's a high-percentage chance you'll hear: "The poor will always be with us."

This loose, partial quote from Jesus is often used as a prophetic assertion regarding perpetual poverty. Many hear it as the rallying sigh of capitulation to the inevitable, and view it as license to develop an attitude of indifference. That assertion is dangerous and damaging.

These words of Jesus are recorded in three of the four gospels. In the accounts of Matthew and Mark, the words emanate from an impromptu, pricey anointing of the Rabbi at a dinner party by an unnamed woman, possibly of questionable character. The disciples and other diners accuse her of a wasteful expression of affection; they don't hesitate to suggest that a more altruistic gesture would have been to sell the precious balm and give the money to the poor, rather than saturating Jesus' dusty scalp. But He sees it as one woman's ultimate demonstration of veneration—the kind reserved solely for a beloved savior.

With His crucifixion looming large, Jesus declares, "The poor you will always have with you, and you can help them any time you want. But you will not always have me" (Mark 14:7). Contrast this with His parting statement to His disciples in Matthew 28:20 when He tells them that He would always be with them, and the conclusion becomes obvious: There at the table in Bethany, Jesus was simply saying that in a little while He would be physically absent from them, and thus this perceptive maiden's expression of worth was completely appropriate.

But there's an interesting Old Testament connection here that suggests Jesus may have been inferring something additional by His always-have-the-poor statement. In Deuteronomy 15, Israel is getting from God, via Moses, another living-life lesson, this time on debt cancellations and caring for their covenant nation. Verses 4 and 5 say, "There should be no poor among you, for in the land the Lord your God is giving you to possess as your inheritance, He will richly bless you, if only you fully obey the Lord your God and are careful to follow all these commands I am giving you today." In other words, be obedient and you will not have a portion of your people permanently poor. Jesus may have been asserting that because of Israel's history of noncompliance with God's commandments, His disciples could expect a lingering legacy of Jewish poverty. He knew His people.

Back in Deuteronomy 15:11, Moses adds another layer to this discussion: "There will always be poor people in the land. Therefore I command you to be openhanded toward your brothers and toward the poor and needy in your land." Having just said that the Israelites wouldn't have poor if they followed God's commandments, it seems like Moses is making a contradictory statement. In all probability, he was saying that even if we have no poor among our people, surely citizens from other nations would come to us for help. Either way, they could count on having poor people in their midst.

For certain, the presence of the poor and Israel's improper response toward them wasn't due to lack of instruction. There are hundreds of references to the needy, weak, lowly, oppressed, and aliens in the Bible, especially in the Old Testament. Passages reveal God's compassion on the poor, detail laws established to protect the poor, and describe blessings and curses associated with treatment of the poor.

In Leviticus 19:9–10, Hebrew farmers are told, "When you reap the harvest of your land, do not reap to the very edges of your field or gather the gleanings of your harvest. Do not go over your vineyard a second time or pick up the grapes that have fallen. Leave them for the poor and the alien." In other words, allow those who can't afford to buy your crops to come onto your property and help themselves to whatever you've missed. Deliberately miss a portion so that it's not just the scraps they're getting—save them some of the Grade-A crops. In the book of Ruth, you might remember that the alien widow was picking up leftovers in the field when she met Boaz, her kinsman redeemer.

Even Solomon, one of the wealthiest men to ever live, shows perceptive insights and gives sterling advice regarding the poor:

Rich and poor have this in common: The Lord is the Maker of them all (Proverbs 22:2).

He who oppresses the poor shows contempt for their Maker,
but whoever is kind to the needy honors God (Proverbs 14:31).

He who is kind to the poor lends to the Lord, and
He will reward him for what He has done (Proverbs 19:17).

Do not exploit the poor because they are poor
and do not crush the needy in court (Proverbs 22:22).

The righteous care about justice for the poor,
but the wicked have no such concern (Proverbs 29:7).

A poor person's farm may produce much food,
but injustice sweeps it all away. (Proverbs 13:23, NLT).
(This confirms that a person's poverty may be the result of someone else's wrongdoing.)

He who gives to the poor will lack nothing,
but he who closes his eyes to them receives many curses (Proverbs 28:27).

If a man shuts his ears to the cry of the poor,
he too will cry out and not be answered (Proverbs 21:13).

And God, whom Scripture describes with many names, claims these attributes as well:
Father to the fatherless, defender of widows (Psalm 68:5)
Protector of the poor (Psalm 12:5)
Rescuer of the poor and fatherless (Job 29:12)
Provider for the poor (Psalm 68:10)
Refuge for the poor (Isaiah 25:4)

Just in reading these few references (a fraction of what's in Scripture), do you get the idea that how we treat the poor—our invisible neighbors—is a big deal? You should. It is a big deal. In fact, you wouldn't be wrong if you said that sensitivity to the poor and God's response to mankind's care of the needy is one of the Bible's central and reoccurring themes.

As the 66 books of the Bible tell the unabridged gospel story, there is account after account describing the weaker being oppressed by the stronger, the disadvantaged being mistreated by the privileged, the few being crushed by the many. Time after time we see God taking up the cause of the offended and unfortunate. In Psalm 72:12–14, we are told that God "…will deliver the needy who cry out, the afflicted who have no one to help. He will take pity on the weak and the needy and save the needy from death. He will rescue them from oppression and violence, for precious is their blood in His sight."

If all of unredeemed mankind is sinful in God's sight and suffer the same exclusion, why are the poor any different? Simply put, God's concern throughout Scripture for the physically deprived is a reoccurring expression of His persistent pity on all who are spiritually depraved.

There are interesting parallels between the utter hopelessness of mankind and the bleak desperation of the poor, albeit on very different levels. God, who is not willing that any should perish but all should come to repentance, is rooting for sinners to accept the Savior, just as He is cheering the poor on to a place of sustainability. And just as mankind is totally dependent on the pardon of an omnipotent God, the poor, with no power of negotiation, are totally at the mercy of those with means. Just as mankind is without hope apart from Jesus' gracious sacrifice, the poor are without hope apart from sacrificial intervention.

Could it be that the poor are a microcosm of the unredeemed?

When a person becomes a child of God, the inherent desire to demonstrate His character finds an obvious outlet among the disadvantaged. Even for neophyte followers of Jesus, the instructions found in Scripture are plain and plentiful. Offering present help and eternal hope to neighbors in need underscores the fact that the Gospel is not as much about life after death as it is life instead of death.

CONNECT

How do you think that the notion of having the poor with us always has influenced society's approach to caring for those in need? Do you think this popular notion has affected the church more than the government?

What verse in the Bible regarding the poor—whether in this chapter or not—speaks most directly to you? Can you explain why?

If you think the practice of not reaping to the "very edges of your field" has any application for today, how would you go about purposefully leaving a margin of your crops, products, profits, time or whatever for the poor? Would that be in addition to tithe?

What are the "rights" of the oppressed and destitute that Psalm 82:3 mentions? How and why does Scripture differentiate between the poor, widows and orphans, and aliens and strangers?

What does it mean that the gospel is not as much about life after death as it is life instead of death? If you believe that, how might it change what you tell people when you describe what it means to be a follower of Jesus?

GO DEEPER
Play Esther O'Connor's version of the song "Poor Wayfaring Stranger," and discuss the words and the haunting melody, particularly in light of this Negro Spiritual or Appalachian Spiritual being an anthem for aliens and strangers in a foreign land. Go to http://www.invisibleneighbors.org/pages/video

## Part Two: Jesus and the Year of Jubilee

The jet bridge was filling up fast with green-tagged bags. I added mine and ducked through the doorway and into the cramped cabin of the Regional jet that would carry me home to Colorado Springs. From the backed-up human column in the aisle I spotted seat 9C—and my eyes immediately darted to 9D. It appeared I would be next to a religious figure in full regalia; I guessed him to be a Hasidic rabbi.

In due course I slid my carryon under seat 8C and sat down; my neighbor in 9D said nothing; he was fully engrossed in a cloth-bound book that appeared to be printed in Hebrew. Its pages held his attention for most of the choppy flight.

As we dropped through the clouds just above the Sangre de Cristo Mountains, he closed the manuscript and turned his attention to the landscape below. I took the opportunity to volunteer my Colorado geographical knowledge and pointed out a few of the prominent peaks and mountain towns. He was appreciative and began to ask questions. During the rest of the descent and approach, I learned that his name was Moshe and that he was from Jerusalem. He had only been to the North America twice previously, once to New York and once to Toronto. Colorado Springs was to be his second stop on a five-city lecture tour, speaking to college students about Kabbalah.

The landing gear lowered and locked into place. I looked at Rabbi Moshe and asked, "Do you know that Colorado Springs is headquarters for more than 100 Christian organizations?"

He nodded vigorously, his curled sidelocks exaggerating the confirmation.

"Yes, I have heard," he added, as if the nodding wasn't a sufficient acknowledgement. "Maybe I will not meet any of the people who work for those places."

I let a few second of silence pass and then said softly, "It's too late. You're talking to one."

Moshe threw his head back and mimed a silent laugh. "It's nice to meet you," he said, punctuating the comment with two sharp slaps to my shoulder. I was certain he meant it.

Moments later I stood in the jet bridge, back to the wall, awaiting the return of the green-tagged bags. Moshe stood across from me. Flanking both of us, shoulder to shoulder, were a dozen or so mum, motionless passengers. Those with only carryons filed steadily between us toward the terminal.

Moshe looked over at me with a quirky smile. "It is like the Red Sea," he said. I shook my head, grinning.

The exodus slowed. Still no gate-checked luggage.

Moshe broke the silence: "So, tell me, why are you Christians so fascinated with Jesus?" Every head in the metal hallway simultaneously turned toward him and then toward me, as if it were a choreographed maneuver. I felt like someone had just switched on a microphone and put it to my mouth.

"Well," I started slowly, "for me…it's because He is such an enigma. Just when you think you have Him figured out, He confounds you with another mystery. He was disarming yet dangerous. He was orthodox but at the same time radical. He didn't choose typical disciples, didn't take them to appropriate places, didn't hang out with popular people, didn't give expected responses. I think that if He physically descended into our culture right now and did what He did in His day, He would cause a stir in the Christian church the likes of which haven't been seen since Martin Luther."

The bags started coming through the door, two at a time; their owners quickly claimed them then hustled off. Moshe waited until I had mine.

"That is a courageous thing for a Christian to say in Colorado Springs," Moshe whispered, half stating, half asking. "Please tell me more of your thoughts on Jesus. I have some time until my ride comes."

For the next 40 minutes we sat in the airport, sipped A&W Root Beer (which I didn't realize was kosher), and talked about Jewish law and Jesus. What follows is a summary of where the conversation went.

I started by talking about the debut of Jesus' ministry in His old neighborhood. The main event was simply a reading of Scripture in His home synagogue. Jesus scanned through the scroll of the prophet Isaiah until He found the passage He wanted to read. He began by saying to those in attendance, "Today this scripture is fulfilled in your hearing." He then read: "The Spirit of the Lord is on me, because He has anointed me to proclaim good news to the poor. He has sent me to proclaim freedom for the prisoners and recovery of sight for the blind, to set the oppressed free, to proclaim the year of the Lord's favor" (Luke 4:18-19).

I suggest that what many Christians don't realize when they read this—unless they follow the trail of microscopic marginal notes—is that the year of the Lord's favor is another name for the Year of Jubilee, an every-50-year occurrence described in Leviticus 25 that God told Moses Israel needed to honor.

Moshe was well versed on the Year of Jubilee. He added wonderful color commentary on the topic.

Every seven years the Israelites were told to have a Sabbatical Year, during which all debts were to be canceled, plus the people were not to plant anything, and not even harvest whatever came up on its own. They were to let the land lay dormant. They could go out into the fields and vineyards and eat whatever grew naturally that year, and were promised that it would be enough—not only for that year, but for the next year when there would be no crops to harvest.

After seven Sabbatical Years came a Year of Jubilee. During the Year of Jubilee, the Sabbatical Year rules were in effect for debts and for planting, harvesting, and storing. But in addition, during the Year of Jubilee, every piece of land had to revert to its original owner, every person had to move back to where his or her family was originally from, and all slaves were set free. We're talking fundamental life changes on every front. It was like reaching in with a straightened paper clip and pushing life's reset button, or like clearing off the Monopoly board: All the houses and apartments went back in the box, all the money went back to the bank, and all the players went back to Go. Israel's whole economy was to be pegged to the Year of Jubilee. It was fascinating proposition.

I told Moshe that I thought the most amazing thing about the Year of Jubilee was that nowhere in Scripture is there any record of Israel ever following it. Perhaps a few families here and there did as it directed, but Israel's corporate quandaries were evidence enough that the Year of Jubilee was basically ignored. Interestingly, the nation known for a plethora of laws and rules and fastidious customs apparently never kept this one particular commandment that had the greatest potential to forever change its collective character. But it's not hard to figure out why.

The Year of the Jubilee would have given the poor a chance to recover. It would have kept wealthy magnates from manipulating others through compounded acquisitions. It would have ingrained into every man, women, and child that all ownership was temporary, that everything belonged to God, and that short-term perspective was the only way to go through life. But rare are those who are willing to give up what they have gathered over a lifetime.

When Jesus read those words from Isaiah—prefaced with "Today this scripture is fulfilled in your hearing"—I suggest to Moshe that Jesus was fundamentally declaring that once again there was hope for the poor, the enslaved, the unhealthy, and the oppressed. Israel may not have adhered to the Year of Jubilee, but by following His teachings, there was a second chance to experience what it offered: a new beginning with new perspective. It would still require a considerable amount of giving on the part of all who followed.

Moshe agreed that Jesus went on to live in a way that shunned long-term wealth. He spent His time with the people who would benefit most from a Year of Jubilee, and through His miracles, He let those same people experience what it would be like to have such a renewal. He even said His kingdom was based on those principles. Certainly there is so much more to Jesus' ministry, but at the core is the concept of unwrapping our arms from around what we think is good in order to embrace that which is infinitely much better.

"I am glad I asked you that question," said Moshe, standing to his feet. We exchanged email addresses.

"I do not believe your Jesus is the Messiah," concluded the rabbi, "but I do believe that if Christians followed His teachings on ownership as we just discussed, other religions would begin to look at Christianity with new eyes."

## CONNECT

In what ways do you think Jesus was radical in His views? Do you think He would cause a stir in your church if He physically spent a Sunday in your services and a Monday night with the governing body?

What do you think Jesus meant when He said in Mark 10:23-29, "It is easier for a camel to go through the eye of a needle than for someone who is rich to enter the kingdom of God?" Why do you think His disciples were so taken aback by Jesus' statements in this passage?

Do you think that Jesus is in some ways like the Year of Jubilee, or do you think He was actually the fulfillment of the Year of Jubilee? If you think He was the fulfillment, what does that say about how He wants you to live?

Do you believe, as some people assert, that Jesus was actually homeless? What does Jesus mean in Luke 9:58 when He says, "Foxes have dens and birds have nests, but the Son of Man has no place to lay his head?"

Are Christians today just as guilty for not fully following Jesus' teachings regarding possessions and the poor as the Israelites were for not keeping the Year of Jubilee?

## GO DEEPER

In your group, pretend that it is 952 B.C. You are living in Israel and the Year of Jubilee is in two years—and the entire nation has to adhere to it. Plan what the next two years would look like in your life. Talk about how it would change not only views about income and expenses, but also about family and possessions. Is there anybody in your group who would relish the Year of Jubilee? What aspects of it make people dig their heels in the hardest?

## Part Three: The Matthew 25 upshot

When ministers and even people in the mainstream want to make a prodigious point about helping the poor, their supporting scripture of choice is certain to be something from Matthew 25:31-46. It seems to be the big gun in the biblical arsenal. Not only does it cover the major conditions of the disadvantaged, it also is specific in naming appropriate responses. What's more, reward and punishment is cited for action or lack thereof. Please take some time to read it right now in a couple of versions and paraphrases.

You'll notice that the daily essentials of food and drink are included in what's to be provided. Clothing is mentioned. Temporary shelter—taking someone in—rounds out the responses to the three basic human needs. Medical care comes next, something people of all economic conditions and ages need. It concludes with companionship, specifically for the prisoner. It definitely is a list of indispensables.

In a Christian culture that seems to be increasingly curious about caring for those in need, Matthew 25:31-46 gets a lot of play. Fragments of the passage frequently appear on church message marquees. Pastors, priests, and sometimes politicians repeatedly quote its popular words. Scores of organizations working for social justice use key phrases from the text on their websites. There is a slew of faith-based corporations— service organizations, networks, coalitions, and foundations—that have Matthew 25 as part of their name. For certain, this New Testament chapter title has become synonymous with anything related to helping the hurting in Jesus' name: "Come join us as we do Matthew 25 work."

These verses, however, present a couple of problems that need to be addressed, particularly as they relate to our conversation about invisible neighbors. The first issue to be resoled has to do with the identity of "the least of these brothers and sisters of mine" in verse 40.

It would be convenient for those working with the poor to be able to inspire others to action by saying that in this passage, Jesus is talking about everyone everywhere who happens to be in need. After all, if humankind was created in God's likeness, and Jesus came in that same likeness and lived a normal (but sinless) human life, then it follows that He could claim the whole human race as "brothers and sisters." And brothers and sisters without life's necessities could qualify as "the least" among us. But that's a leap that doesn't fly with a lot of Bible scholars.

The book of Matthew is called the Jewish gospel, meaning it was written by a Jew for a Jewish audience. Matthew quotes regularly from the Old Testament and uses titles for Jesus that are thoroughly Jewish, such as Messiah and Son of David. Throughout the book, the mission of Jesus and the disciples is directed toward "the lost sheep of the house of Israel." For this reason, you'll find some who say that "the least of these brothers and sisters of mine" is referring only to Jews. But with the onset of the church, that barrier breaks down quickly.

A more reasonable interpretation, based on context, is that "the least of these brothers and sisters of mine" is talking about followers of Jesus—those who share the same Father in heaven. In Mark 3:35, Jesus says the person who obeys God's will is his brother and sister, and certainly not everyone everywhere is following faithfully after God.

To take it one step further, with comparisons to language used in Matthew 10:40-42—where Jesus is concluding His remarks to the disciples that He is grooming to spread His message—a very strong argument could be made that "the least of these brothers and sisters of mine" is referring to followers of Jesus, and specifically those who are involved in doing His work, such as pastors and missionaries. Historically, many of them have been in poverty and prison, and a lot face those conditions today.

So if the "least of these" in Matthew 25 is contextually talking about Jesus' envoys, does that mean non-Christians are left out in the cold when it comes to this continuum of care? Definitely not.

In regard to the identity of the recipients of care in Matthew 25, think priority and not exclusivity. An example of this principle might be found on the battlefield. If you were a combatant in a firefight that resulted in military as well as civilian wounded, as a good soldier you would tend first to the needs of your comrades in arms, and then move on to help the injured populace. In other words, while Matthew 25 is probably an admonition to care for those delivering Jesus' message, there is nothing in the text that says it is to stop there. In fact, everything else in Scripture indicates that it's only a starting point. There is certainly a concentric circle not too far removed from the heart of the matter that holds within its border all of the poor in our midst. The Message puts a spin on Galatians 6:10 that corroborates this perspective: "Right now, therefore, every time we get the chance, let us work for the benefit of all, starting with the people closest to us in the community of faith.

The second issue to be resolved with Matthew 25:31-46 is the conundrum of consequence. If you read the passage and take it solely at face value, you could conclude that Jesus is propagating a gospel of works.

The grandiose orchestration of separating the sheep and the goats in verses 31-33 shows that this isn't some incidental commendation or condemnation. It is of final judgment proportions—the ultimate determination of destiny for character-distinguishing behavior. That is confirmed to be the case when the one group is ultimately rewarded with kingdom inheritance, and the other group winds up with unending suffering.

This passage appears to be saying that because you cared for people in a certain way you get the ultimate reward: everlasting life. And because you didn't provide the care, you get ultimate punishment: everlasting death.

However, the rest of Scripture does not support that. Salvation through grace alone—sola gratia in Latin—was one of the five pillars of the Protestant Reformation and

later affirmed by the Catholic Church. Countless volumes have been written on this important Christian doctrine. The very familiar passage of Ephesians 2:8-9 says quite plainly that grace trumps works. How then should we read the action and reward (or inaction and punishment) nexus of Matthew 25:31-46?

It's fairly basic. The "goats" in the story have never availed themselves of Jesus' saving grace—and their actions show it. On the other hand, the "sheep" are already recipients of His gift. That's a given. Thus, the "sheep's" response to the "least of these" has nothing at all to do with the procurement of their salvation; it is very simply the proof of their salvation. That is to say, if you are a genuine follower of Jesus, service to the "least of these"—ministers of the gospel first, and then all of the invisible neighbors who come next—will simply be second nature.

It's interesting that Jesus contrasts sheep with goats to represent those who followed and those who didn't, respectively. Sheep may be slow and skittish, but once sheep learn a pattern, as a rule, they lock into it and follow faithfully. Goats are more independent and tend to do their own thing. While independence might be an admired lifestyle in our Western world, it's not a livestock trait that pleases a shepherd.

The sheep metaphor seems to serve as a final punctuation to the parable: Jesus isn't talking about occasional adherence to His wishes. Rather, He's talking about a submissive existence in which serving becomes synonymous with following.

## CONNECT

How does James 2:14-24 help us understand Matthew 25:31-46? Do you think that the interlinking of faith and works is fully understood in most churches today?

In this present day, how do we care for ministers of the gospel in need, or does that tenet only apply when there is persecution present? Could ensuring that a pastor is paid a respectable wage be counted as Matthew 25-type care?

What does Matthew 10:41-42 communicate about offering hospitality to preachers and missionaries? What is the reward that is mentioned?

Would you guess that the reason most people don't respond to the needs of "one of the least of these" is lack of resources, fear of continuing obligation, or simply not knowing what to do? How should the church train its people in this regard?

How many coats do you personally own? If you felt led to give one away to someone in need, what would it take for you to select your nicest one as opposed to one that was old and tattered?

## GO DEEPER

Listen to/watch Sherri Youngward's song titled "Broadway." Discuss as a group where you find Matthew 25 in the lyrics. Go to http://www.invisibleneighbors.org/pages/video

_____

_____

_____

_____

_____

_____

_____

_____

_____

_____

_____

_____

_____

_____

_____

_____

# GROUP PRAYER & PRAISE SHEET

Briefly share your prayer requests as a group, recording the requests below. Remember to record any answers to prayer below.

| PERSON | PRAYER REQUEST | PRAISE RESPONSE |
|--------|----------------|-----------------|
|  |  |  |
|  |  |  |
|  |  |  |
|  |  |  |
|  |  |  |
|  |  |  |
|  |  |  |
|  |  |  |
|  |  |  |
|  |  |  |
|  |  |  |
|  |  |  |
|  |  |  |
|  |  |  |
|  |  |  |
|  |  |  |

Engage: Watch Session Five on video

If you are becoming more aware of the neighbors in need throughout your community, and you are realizing that their presence and circumstances are not part of a fleeting phenomenon, you have four choices:

You can close your eyes to them and hope they become invisible again.
You can assume the government—some national or local program
—will provide the assistance they need.
You can pray that the church—specifically a congregation that's socially minded
—will extend some measure of care for them.
You can believe the Bible's mandate for tendering care applies to you (and your family)
and begin to extend Christian hospitality to those within your reach.

The term Christian hospitality has been part of the evangelical vocabulary for eons. What's remarkable is that very few prominent religious leaders have ever attempted to define it, particularly considering the important part hospitality played in the early Christian church.

Original, authentic Christian hospitality was actually a lifestyle that emerged immediately after Pentecost. The last few verses of Acts chapter 2 tell us that as the outflowing of the Spirit produced convicting preaching and miraculous results in their midst, all of the believers met together in one place and shared everything they had. They sold their property and possessions and gave the money to those in need. They also shared their meals with great joy and generosity. (See Acts 2:42-46.) The common themes were community, benevolence, accommodation, and celebration. Who wouldn't want to be part of that?

This outpouring of home-based charity in early Acts was just one of the ways the elders and those new to the movement obeyed Jesus, who before His death told His followers to "Love one another. As I have loved you, so you must love one another. By this everyone will know that you are my disciples, if you love one another" (John 13:34–35). In other words, hospitality was how they lived out love on a daily basis, particularly at a time and place where there were constant outbreaks of conviction and conversion, and consequently so much need. By the way, Jesus hasn't rescinded that commandment.

Later on in the book of Acts, we find that hospitality was also how followers of Jesus cared for their leaders who traveled extensively, encouraging and instructing the believers, and inviting others into the faith. Inns were notoriously dirty and dangerous places in those days. To take people you respected to an inn said you really didn't respect them all that much. Instead, you took them home with you so you could be certain of their care and safety. More than that, the followers of Jesus knew that to refuse Jesus' messengers was to refuse Jesus' message. (See Luke 10:10–16.) In some of the Epistles, those who exemplified abundant hospitality were identified by name and esteemed.

As the church grew in the first and second centuries, faith was often forged in the environment of hospitality. Christianity was a home-centered movement in those days—more table-based than altar-predicated. Countless converts to this new faith learned about Jesus from mealtime discussions—as well as from the courteous treatment they received—in the abodes of those who had recently come on board. The New Testament documents churches that met in the homes of Priscilla and Aquila (Romans 16:3-5) and Nympha (Colossians 4:15), to mention just two.

The followers of Jesus didn't rent public space for meetings. That could have been a costly proposition in more ways than one; as time went on, most Christians had to go into hiding just to talk about their beliefs.

The commonplace, comfortable religion that Christianity is today in most of the Western world is a far cry from that fledgling faith of the first century. We have been blessed with spacious sanctuaries, comfortable classrooms, and well-equipped multi-purpose centers to worship, learn, and fellowship. But one cannot help but wonder if abundance and institutionalization have eliminated the desire for (and reliance on) the kind of radical hospitality that made the New Testament church the powerful, compelling, and unpredictable entity that it was.

Spin the globe and look at places where Jesus' work is flourishing and you'll find that hospitality is a core component there. The ministry is sometimes clandestine and dangerous, and usually unsophisticated, but hospitality is that irreplaceable catalyst for growth.

Today, throughout North America, people are credited with exhibiting Christian hospitality if they hand out welcome packets to Sunday-morning visitors or regularly host youth group functions at their home. These are indeed considerate endeavors, but fall far short of the New Testament model.

To better understand what Christian hospitality is, you have to understand what it is not.

It is not entertaining. Entertaining has presentation overtones, making it as much about displaying yourself—house, family, or accomplishments—as serving someone else. That presentation aspect shows up in statements such as: "As soon as we get the carpets shampooed, we'll have a game night and invite our friends." Or maybe: "As soon as I perfect that lamb chop recipe, we'll invite that new family at church over for dinner."

Entertaining is mostly about inviting people into your house. Hospitality is about inviting people into your life. True Christian hospitality doesn't really mind if the dishes aren't done or the mail is stacked on the counter or the pillows on the couch aren't fully fluffed. It centers on the needs of others. Everything else is incidental.

Christian hospitality is not gender-bound. More specifically, it is not a woman's responsibility. Our culture leans toward the woman being the primary host of the home—unless a backyard grill is involved—and thus the purveyor of any related hospitality. Investing in the lives of others requires no gender-specific skills. In fact, there are some hospitality-related practices for which men are better suited, such as heavy service chores and man-to-man conversations and counseling. We just have to get beyond the longstanding lie that hospitality is a woman's work.

Hospitality is not something to be extended just to friends. Now this is where things can get a bit foreboding. Home invasions and swindles and abductions certainly do occur, but by using common sense and taking proper precautions, the chances of being victimized by a sober, balanced stranger to whom you are offering hospitality are miniscule.

Sadly, in the interest of expedience, North Americans today tend to take the innocuous route and steer clear of all strangers. Radical Christian hospitality doesn't offer that option. Moreover, it doesn't discriminate and decide, "I'll offer hospitality if they are clean…if they don't smell…if they don't smoke…if they are white…if they are citizens…if they speak English…if they aren't living in sin…if they don't have a prison record…if they show interest in Christianity…if their schedule works with mine…if…if…if."

There is no shortage of churches today proclaiming themselves to be warm and welcoming, but the whole cannot genuinely bring to bear what the individual parts do not possess. Invisible neighbors do not want to be absorbed into a congregation of perky people; they long to be taken in by compassionate individuals who willingly share their provisions and perspectives, homes and hearts. Going forward, the churches that will make a real difference in our world—and maybe even the ones that will survive—are the ones that can rekindle a perspective on hospitality like they had in the first-century church.

Arthur Sutherland closes his book titled I Was a Stranger (Abingdon Press, 2006) with observations about a photo of a young hitchhiker standing on the island of a busy street.

"Tall and gaunt, she bore the weary expression that we so often see carried by those who feel themselves on the margin of life. Clumped beside her feet were her bound possessions that appeared to be as rumpled as what she wore. All of this was, unfortunately, rather ordinary. Folks of her band are as common as the cars that passed by her. What made the picture compelling was the sign she held. Written on a piece of cardboard was the word Anywhere. She asked not for Los Angeles, New York, or Miami. She asked not for home or to be taken away from home. All of this was a road too far. She simply asked, dare I say begged, to be taken not away, but to be taken in. If this is the case, that she wanted to be taken in and not just away, then she represents those who Jesus calls us to see. Hospitality is the practice by which the church stands or falls."

CONNECT

How does the radical hospitality of Barnabas, as demonstrated in Acts 4:36-37 strike you? Do you think the fact that Barnabas laid the money at the apostles' feet indicates that it was done in a humble manner and may have been initially anonymous?

Would the Underground Railroad of the nineteenth century be as successful as it was if it had to operate in the 21st century? If you said no, what would have to change to make it successful, or have societal changes taken that kind of radical hospitality away from us forever?

In the prerequisites for church leaders, detailed in 1 Timothy 3:2, is the requirement to be hospitable on the same par as the others listed, or is it optional? Are people who say they don't have the "gift" of hospitality off the hook in this whole area?

When Hebrews 13:2 cautions us not to forget to show hospitality to strangers, does that include people who may be on the streets? Do you know anyone who thinks he or she has entertained an angel through hospitality, and if so, how does that individual describe the experience?

What programs or services does your church offer that resembles early New Testament hospitality? Are they programs and services that attract men as well as women?

GO DEEPER

Watch/listen to the song "Be Our Guest" from Disney's Beauty and the Beast, and discuss what elements of it skew the image that most people today have regarding hospitality. Go to http://www.invisibleneighbors.org/pages/video

# Part Two: Community, then houses

Keith set out from Minneapolis in his late teens, in search of warmth and whatever came next. He moved to Albuquerque and looked for employment, but not too intently.

At first he stayed in seedy motels and public shelters, but eventually slept on the streets, covering himself with cardboard and rags when cold, and nothing at all when not. Alcohol and drugs became a regular part of his life, although he rarely scored enough to stay high for any period of time. At 28, he had no work résumé and no legitimate job skills. Panhandling and petty larceny kept him alive. All of his earthly possessions could fit into the pockets of his pants.

Darryl was 43 and did have a résumé. He earned a B.S. in accounting from an unsung college near Cleveland, and then worked for a while in a bank. That's where he met Bonnie. They married after a brief courtship.

An offer from a friend to be the bookkeeper at a real estate office in Raleigh appeared to be a better opportunity, so they moved there with one child and one on the way. The job worked out; the marriage didn't. Bonnie left and moved back to Ohio with the kids. He plodded along in North Carolina until the bottom fell out of the real estate market and he was let go.

Unemployment couldn't cover alimony, child support, a mortgage, and his personal expenses. He lost his battles with the finance company and with depression. The house went back to the bank and Darryl went to a homeless shelter.

Although they had never met, Keith and Darryl were soon to have a common experience: They both learned about Housing First—a government-funded concept that puts homeless people in houses with the philosophy that once someone is in stable housing, all of life's other issues have a better chance of getting worked out.

Without an income and with a history of substance abuse, Keith qualified for a free residence under the Shelter Plus Care Program, managed by the U.S. Department of Housing and Urban Development. He was given the keys to an apartment and was told to see a substance-abuse counselor weekly. The counselor had an unmanageable caseload. He and Keith met once.

The young drifter stayed by himself for the first few nights, and then, one by one, some of his street pals joined him—and brought their stashes. Housing First, for all of its good intentions, simply enabled him to bring the party indoors.

One night Keith stood in his kitchen trying to determine what was different. Something. He finally was able to focus on the fact that the refrigerator had vanished. He had no idea where it went or who was responsible, but for some reason there was an abundance of party supplies the rest of that week.

Darryl received Section 8 assistance to get his house. Section 8 is a common reference to Section 8 of the frequently amended United States Housing Act of 1937, which authorizes rental-housing payments to private landlords to make up the difference for those who can't afford to pay them full fare. Darryl found he could get out of the shelter for just 30 percent of what was left of his unemployment check after the courts collected what they wanted.

He moved into a one-bedroom walk-up without character, curtains, or knickknacks. A 5-by-7 photo of him with his daughters filled the only frame in the entire place. Darryl felt the apartment's décor was an apt representation of his soul—bleak and empty. Although he had a bed, he slept on the sofa. That, plus the toilet and television, were the only things that got daily use. Occasionally the freezer, microwave, and trashcan came into play.

Without today's government-subsidized housing, the number of people literally sleeping on the streets would be fifty times greater than it is right now. The Housing First initiative has helped many people find a permanent place, and, eventually, their way in the world.

But for every one of those, there's a Keith and a Darryl who don't need a house as much as they need a community. In time they will want and need four walls, a roof, and a floor. Right now they need to be in a place with people who can surround them with love, cover them with medical and psychological care, and give them the solid footing of Jesus' life-changing message. Community—more specifically, Christian community—can engender new life in a way physical structures cannot.

St. Patrick had it figured out. His strategy for introducing Ireland to Jesus' claims was totally based on the concept of community. George Hunter does an excellent job of detailing it in The Celtic Way of Evangelism (Abingdon Press, 2000).

Born in England, the teenage Patrick was kidnapped, taken to Ireland, and sold into slavery. He escaped, but after becoming a priest he felt called to go back to Ireland to the people he had come to know and love during his bondage. At that time, Ireland was a country of overlapping tribes living in what Hunter called "rural sprawl." The land lacked solid civic structure. To connect with the people, Patrick built little monastic communities at key intersections of commerce.

These spiritual settlements were different from other monastic communities found east of the Isles at that time. For one thing, you didn't have to be a convert to Christianity to move in. Also, priests were present but lay leadership was predominant. Every day, inhabitants worked out issues of life in the context of faith. Everyone was invited to worship even though some in the gatherings did not yet comprehend the God being worshiped.

All of this was core to Patrick's concept that establishing community and bringing people into fellowship needed to precede engagement in meaningful faith conversations, and certainly any public commitment. In time, numerous residents affirmed their new belief and marked it through an appropriate ritual. They were then candidates to help form new monastic communities elsewhere in Ireland.

In contrast to the philosophy of spiritual restoration that is about helping people believe so they can belong, the community approach that St. Patrick took—and the one that works well with invisible neighbors—is more concerned with helping people belong so they can believe.

What does that look like today? It involves engagement—making eye contact and giving a you-are-accepted smile. It involves communication—talking to and not down to. It involves invitations—for coffee in a local café, for a walk around the block, for a salmon dinner done on the backyard grill. The rest generally falls into place by itself.

Without a doubt, many invisible neighbors—like Keith, for example—are not ready to leave their enabling peer networks and embrace faith-centered community. Critical intervention and treatment must take place first. But when they are ready—like Darryl might be—the acceptance into community can be a blessing to all parties, further demonstrating that community, then houses, is how people are restored.

## CONNECT

Considering all they have been through, does your heart go out more to Keith or Darryl? How do you think Jesus would answer that question, and would His answer make you want to rethink yours?

What Housing First initiatives are located in your area? How can your church be involved with a Housing First initiative and help bring community to those living there?

How is community different than a "clan" (as discussed in Session 1)? How do you keep a community from turning into a clan?

What does Paul's farewell address to the elders in Ephesus, found in Acts 20:16-38, say about the importance of community? How strong is your spiritual community, and how do you contribute to its success?

In a post-Christian world where fewer and fewer people have a "faith upbringing," does the Celtic style of evangelism (where fellowship comes before rather than after conversion) seem to make sense? Does the phrase "belonging before believing" bother you in any way?

## GO DEEPER

Watch/listen to George Hunter describe the Roman style of evangelism as opposed to the Celtic style of evangelism, and discuss it as a group. Talk about how invisible neighbors might be more receptive to the Celtic style.

Go to http://www.invisibleneighbors.org/pages/video

## Part Three: Christ, then programs

The glass-encased signboard hanging in the church narthex said it all. At the top, the embedded white plastic letters laid out the coming week's evening meetings:

| | |
|---|---|
| Monday | Alcoholics Anonymous |
| Tuesday | Abused Spouses |
| Wednesday | Eating Disorders |
| Thursday | Say No To Drugs |
| Friday | Teen Suicide Watch |
| Saturday | Soup Kitchen |

Underneath this unsettling schedule was the subject of the approaching Sunday's morning sermon:

"America's Joyous Future"

The title of the message, viewed in light of the meeting lineup, suggests one of two things: Either the church leaders are exceedingly optimistic, or they are totally clueless.

While the advertised sessions might seem depressing to some—particularly those who have had to deal with one or more of the topics being talked about—the issues are commonplace in our society. In fact, the church's meeting planner could probably produce a calendar for the entire month in which a different human condition or social disorder is addressed every night, and not duplicate any of the classes.

This is not to minimize the fact that there are many individuals with valid disorders stemming from physiological problems. Naturally, medical attention is necessary in such situations. And there are people in the strong grip of powerful drugs. Detox and serious rehab are required in these cases.

But so much of what shows up on the streets today is destructive behavior caused by unimaginable emotional clutter. As a result, we find no shortage of programs offered by colleges, nonprofit organizations, government agencies, and even churches, all designed to help people deal with their circumstances and recover from their bad choices. Unfortunately, the one thing that many courses have in common is that the focus is on fixing the obvious symptoms and not the underlying cause.

Cause, from a spiritual perspective, comes back to one basic issue.

In John 8, Jesus is telling some fellow Jews who think they are the children of God that they really have a different father. In verses 43 and 44 He engages them: "Why is my language not clear to you? Because you are unable to hear what I say. You belong to your father, the devil, and you want to carry out your father's desires. He was a murderer from the beginning, not holding to the truth, for there is no truth in him. When he lies, he speaks his native language, for he is a liar and the father of lies."

If you want to address the cause and not symptoms, you have to address Satan's lies—lies that say I'm not good enough the way I am, I could never be forgiven for what I've done, I couldn't ever forgive what's been done to me, I am not loved by anyone, I need more than what I have. I couldn't ever be happy without him…her…this…that.

When people do not have spiritual grounding to help them distinguish truth from lies, the lies become larger than life and set them on a course that's hard to reverse. The Apostle Paul tells the Corinthians just why it's hard: "In their case the god of this world has blinded the minds of the unbelievers, to keep them from seeing the light of the gospel of the glory of Christ, who is the image of God" (2 Corinthians 4:4 ESV).

Unfortunately, even believers, while set free from Satan's power, can be deceived. As followers of Jesus, we put our hope in him for protection from this present world's perils and for our prepared place in a future world. Still, life is messy, and we all deal with our share of stuff. Sometimes the stuff can engulf us more than we ever imagined, opening our ears to lies and our hearts to errant choices.

But if Satan's lies—and our sinful response—are the cause of great anguish, regardless of whom we are talking about, it follows that Christ's truth is the cure. When that cure is dispensed in a community of hospitality, the prognosis for recovery is very good.

So, what exactly is Christ's truth? It's the fact that there really is a better life. John 10:10 from The Message puts it this way: "A thief [a.k.a. liar] is only there to steal and kill and destroy. I came so they can have real and eternal life, more and better life than they ever dreamed of."

For an unbeliever to receive this real and eternal life, he or she needs to come to terms with God's redemption story. (See John 3:16-17 and Romans 10:9-10.) Then he or she needs to acknowledge that for the work of Jesus to be personally life transforming, old attitudes and habits must be abandoned; new perspectives and practices must be adopted. It's all about faith verified by actions. (See Ephesians 2:8–9 and James 2:14–26.) Over time, faith and actions develop a direct correlation: Each has a wonderful way of increasing the other—and producing that "more and better" life.

Our invisible neighbors simply need to know about this life, and have it explained to them in nonthreatening encounters.

A college friend and I arranged to rendezvous in the lobby of the Latham Hotel in Philadelphia. I arrived the same time as his text, which said he was running late by 40 minutes. With this unexpected interlude in my schedule, a visit to the Belgium waffle and coffee shop, right across the street, seemed like a fine idea. A few minutes later I emerged with a covered cup in my right hand and a small bag in my left, and then strolled around the corner and one block down to Rittenhouse Square, a historic center-city park, surrounded by luxury high-rise residences.

The winding walkways under the oaks and locusts directed mostly well-dressed people, some evidently running behind time, which made others look as if they were in slow motion. On the grassy patches were students, spread out on blankets with books and laptops. The benches that paralleled the footpaths held mostly elderly people, feeding pigeons and reminiscing.

By the goat statue, I noticed a girl, probably in her teens, curled up on the concrete wall. The fact that she was wearing two coats and resting her head on a grungy, bulging backpack provided my hunch that she didn't live above the park in one of the upscale condos.

She sat up when I sat down across from her, but didn't speak. I greeted her and offered the second waffle in my bag. She shrugged but reached for it. That act launched our conversation.

I surmised that Kelly was a runaway. She didn't give many clues to her background but did mention Toronto twice. I asked her where she was headed; that produced another shrug. She finished the waffle and wiped her hands on her jeans. I looked over into eyes that had seen far more miles and misery than her years should have allowed. I asked Kelly if there weren't people worried about her, wondering where she was.

She stared right past me into the park and, without any expression in her voice, uttered five heartbreaking words: "I don't matter to anybody."

Kelly believed the lies. She represents so many of our invisible neighbors who slink in and out of the shadows of life, merely existing, absolutely convinced that nobody cares about them.

To people in Kelly's predicament, professional counseling and carefully administered programs will probably come into play at some point. But first these individuals need to hear and believe Christ's truth. And according to John 8:32, when they experience that truth, it will set them free in a way they have never experienced.

The invitation to journey toward truth starts with something as simple as this: "Kelly, you matter to Jesus, and because I am one of His followers, you matter to me. There's a better road than the one you're traveling, and I can lead you to it. For starters, there's a wonderful young couple I know who live down on Delancey Place. You'd really like them. I know them well enough to know that they would love to put you up for a few days. Are you interested?"

After what seemed like an eternity of silence Kelly responded. With a hint of hope in her voice she asked, "How far is Delancey Place?"

## CONNECT

If your church were to offer the programs and services that were mentioned on the signboard, how much of the enrollment would come from inside the church versus outside the church? Why do you think it is that people in the church have a harder time talking about their issues than people on the streets?

Would you concur that believing Satan's lies are a root cause for the emotional distress that affects so many people living on the streets, or is that just an oversimplification? Why would alcohol and drugs go hand-in-hand with their emotional conditions?

As a follower of Jesus, in what ways do you think you have "more and better life" than someone who isn't one of His followers? Without using "church speak," how would you describe to an invisible neighbor what to expect if he or she chooses to follow Jesus?

What characteristics of Jesus do you think would be most attractive to a runaway? In light of Hebrews 13:3, as paraphrased in The Message, how would you start to relate to a victim of domestic abuse?

What do you think it is about the couple who lived on Delancey Place that would cause the writer to assume it wouldn't be a problem for Kelly to stay with them? How many people do you know like that?

## GO DEEPER

Listen to/watch the video of Lou Fellingham and a church choir singing the song "In Christ Alone." As a group, go over each line of the song and talk about how it relates to the subject of Christ before programs. Go to http://www.invisibleneighbors.org/pages/video

ALTERNATE: Break up into groups of two or three and attend various classes on addiction recovery, stress management, and the like. When you get back together, talk about what you learned, what you thought was valuable, and what you thought wasn't.

# SESSION FIVE NOTES

# GROUP PRAYER & PRAISE SHEET

Briefly share your prayer requests as a group, recording the requests below. Remember to record any answers to prayer below.

| PERSON | PRAYER REQUEST | PRAISE RESPONSE |
|--------|----------------|-----------------|
|        |                |                 |
|        |                |                 |
|        |                |                 |
|        |                |                 |
|        |                |                 |
|        |                |                 |
|        |                |                 |
|        |                |                 |
|        |                |                 |
|        |                |                 |
|        |                |                 |
|        |                |                 |
|        |                |                 |
|        |                |                 |
|        |                |                 |
|        |                |                 |

Engage: Watch Session Six on video

# MISSIONS TO THE RESCUE

## PART ONE: A PERFECT PLACE TO START

Most big cities have a skid row—an area beset with flophouses, crack houses, rundown bars, and abandoned buildings. It's where the observable homeless tend to congregate, often sitting or laying on the sidewalks, or traversing the concrete like zombies on patrol. It's a place where raw emotions rest precariously close to the surface.

Sometimes skid row is called just that; sometimes it goes by another name, like the Tenderloin District in San Francisco or the Downtown Eastside in Vancouver or the Bowery in New York City (although gentrification has changed or is changing some of these places). In other cities, the observable homeless are constantly on the move and show up unpredictably in unexpected places.

But just because homeless people are observable doesn't mean they are seen.

Paul and Debbie's 22-year-old son Ryan dropped out of college his junior year. He left the dorm and moved straight to the streets. The couple couldn't figure out what brought about this devastating change in their boy. Guilt? Depression? Drugs? Heartbroken, they tried to maintain contact, but soon learned that staying in touch with a transient is a futile pursuit.

One October day, after receiving a tip from a family friend who chanced upon Ryan while in a certain metropolitan area on business, Paul took off from work and drove four hours to that city to try and locate his son. He started at skid row—a place he had always known was there but had never really known too much about. He had been afraid of what he heard went on in such a tough part of town, and he had never really had a reason to be there.

But this day was different.

Paul took a deep breath and then his first apprehensive steps in the direction of the local humanity. Half a block later he came to a bus stop bench. There, flat on his back, was a young man under a fanned-out Sunday paper. Paul peeled back the newsprint and looked into his eyes. Not Ryan. Across the street was a body in a doorway, partially walled in by plastic bags filled with worthless odds and ends. He roused and rolled the startled man over and studied the bearded face. Not Ryan either. On the corner on a steam vent stood two men talking, both enveloped by a faint plume of warm fog. Paul circled them looking for a familiar feature. Neither was Ryan. In the adjacent alley was a makeshift cardboard tent with two feet sticking out. Getting down on his knees, Paul peered in and called his son's name. The man sat up. Still no Ryan.

He spent the next two and a half hours looking at homeless men, as opposed to looking them over. When he called Debbie to report in, he didn't have the news she wanted to hear, but he told her something that affected both of them deeply: "Today I saw dozens of men—men who, in the past, were just bodies that blended into the urban landscape.

But it's like the landscape came alive today and these people suddenly became real. I didn't find our son…but I found a lot of other people's sons. While we're waiting for Ryan to come back to us, I think we need to do something to help these guys who are out here."

An epiphany like Paul's generally comes after a poignant experience. But when the emotion dissipates, what's left is the daunting task of actually caring for desperate and destitute people. And it can seem overwhelming.

How does someone not particularly streetwise learn what to do first, or what never to do? Where can a small group go to get trained in how to properly care for invisible neighbors? Are there people who have an edge in experience when it comes to serving hungry, homeless, abused, and addicted people in Jesus' name?

All three questions find answers in ministries called gospel rescue missions. There are gospel rescue missions in most major cities in North America—sometimes more than one. But you probably won't find their buildings in an upscale section of a downtown. Their neighborhoods are less lit, less lively, and more unsettled. Yet despite their lackluster locations, they are vibrant places of promise.

They are havens of hope for the lost and lonely who call the street home. Inside their facilities they have hot food, clean clothing, temporary shelter, caring staff, and the possibility of a more abundant life.

Gospel rescue missions have a long history of providing lifelines for those drowning in the waves of adversity and undertow of addiction. For more than a century, they have been keeping watch on the waterfront of despair, and countless thousands of men, women, and children have been saved in every sense of the word.

Gospel is part of their name because their leaders are compelled foremost by the instructions of Jesus to actively care for those in need, and to introduce them to the liberating good news of His kingdom and all it represents. Their name includes rescue, because delivering those in need from danger is the critical and consuming first part of a sometimes slow but always exciting journey that leads to new desires, new choices, and a new direction in life.

The word missions is in their name because those in need see each of these structures as a bastion of protection and a refuge from fatigue and failure. In that way, gospel rescue missions are like those Southwestern sanctuaries built by pioneering padres long ago.

Gospel rescue missions provide several levels of hospitality. The most basic missions have what's called a day room—a place for people to get out of the heat, cold, or wet weather. There is always someone to talk to for spiritual advice and referrals. Some missions expand their day room and add a feeding program, almost always offering lunch, and sometimes breakfast and supper. More often than not, a chapel program takes place on the property. At some missions, attendance is required in order to obtain assistance, adding a touch of tough regimentation to the often non-structured schedules of the guest; at other missions, chapel is optional. It depends on the mission leaders' philosophy.

Sheltering is the next level of hospitality. It is usually divided into two categories: emergency and long-term. In the former, more rudimentary model, guests are given showers and overnight accommodations, usually in a dorm setting in order to accommodate as many people as possible. Naturally, men and women are housed separately. Most are there to escape the extremes of the elements or domestic violence. Emergency shelter stays are rarely more than a month.

Long-term sheltering provides the guest with a more stable situation, plus it gives staff an opportunity to determine individuals needs and offer services on a deeper level. Sadly, the fastest growing population needing long-term sheltering is women with children. But single women, single men, men with children, and intact families all benefit from this valuable service that gospel rescue missions provide.

In a long-term shelter situation, continuing health care is generally available, sometimes done on site or possibly through a partnership with a clinic or university extension service. Childcare is available for guests studying for their GEDs, going through job-skill training, or starting employment. The concept of saving money is stressed so guests can get on (or back on) their feet and eventually rent their own place. Daily group Bible studies and one-on-one counseling is how the all-important spiritual component envelops the program.

The next level of hospitality is addiction recovery (although some specialized missions do only this). Chemical addictions are the most common, although other life-controlling addictions are also addressed. Addiction recovery programs can be as short as six months and as long as two years. A one-year program is pretty standard. Guests can count on a strict schedule and closely controlled environment, at least at first. Scripture provides the framework for intense counseling and life-skill classes. Regular chapel services round out the faith experience and advance worship to a place of prominence in everyday life.

Some missions go on to develop a social enterprise initiative, like a culinary arts institute, retail operation, manufacturing company, or community service corps, all of which can provide those in the latter stages of an addiction recovery program with valuable hands-on job training. This can make a significant statement on a résumé that might otherwise be void of work experience.

The most multifaceted gospel rescue missions offer housing as the last stage of hospitality, including transitional housing that guests progressing from a long-term shelter or addiction recovery program can inhabit until they are prepared to acquire their own places. Affordable housing is the last level. It's for guests ready to live on their own but not yet in a position to pay the going rate for rent or make a down payment.

As you can see, while gospel rescue missions are known by only one "r" word, they are really about four:

    **Rescue**—pulling people to safety from adverse conditions, and from choices and habits that lead to damaged health and death

    **Redemption**—presenting people with a gospel that is about life transformation in Jesus and the reclamation of His creation

    **Rehabilitation**—helping people break the bonds of addiction and desperate behavior, and experience a life of healing and wholeness

    **Re-assimilation**—preparing people to dwell in community, and to have meaningful roles that lead to stability and missional living

For more than 100 years, gospel rescue missions have been the unsung heroes of street ministry. Volumes have been written on the life-changing work they have done, but they cannot function without volunteers—followers of Jesus who are not afraid to step forward and be counted on to work with other people's sons and daughters when they are at their lowest.

## CONNECT

How much time have you spent observing people on skid row or another such place where homeless gather? What were your initial impressions?

While searching for Ryan, what are some of the things you think went through Paul's mind as he observed homeless men in their surroundings? In what ways might it be more difficult for a woman to endure living on the streets in such a setting?

Why do you think some people seem content to be chronically homeless and even resist people's efforts to help them? What might it take to connect with such people and provide them with assistance?

What are your thoughts about homeless people who have spent years on the streets and know how to "play the system," getting all they can from the government and groups providing them assistance, and failing to take responsibility for anything? Do they deserve any of the help they receive?

What aspects of gospel rescue missions' efforts is the most fascinating to you? What aspects would you question and possibly challenge?

## GO DEEPER

As a group, go to a skid row in your city, or a larger city near you. Walk the streets and interact with some of the people. Make a list of questions to ask them (without coming across like you are interrogating). Take some backpacks full of new socks and distribute them to people who desire them. When you get back together, discuss your experience. NOTE: If this will be a new experience for most in your group, have someone with experience in such a setting talk about dos and don'ts before you go.

## Part Two: Your Invitation for involvement

So here you are, wondering what you've gotten yourself into with this Invisible Neighbors thing. Well unfortunately (or fortunately), this isn't just another study that calls you to greater resolve and more fervent prayer. Invisible Neighbors is in fact a call to action—a call to understand the times, understand the needs, and understand Scripture's mandate, and then make a difference in your neighborhood.

Most North American followers of Jesus, like the rest of the population, are exceedingly busy and constantly on the go. Not too many are seriously searching for one more thing to do. We know what we should be doing, but trying to fit it into what we are already doing is beyond difficult. We may sincerely desire fruitful ministry involvement, but with ever-present over-commitment in our lives, it's so much easier to "mail it in"—send a check or electronic donation—than it is to get physically involved, particularly in something that pushes us outside of our comfort zones.

This is not a suggestion to reconsider financial contributions. Money is the oil that keeps the motors of ministry from seizing up. Rather, this is a reminder that giving does not absolve one from going. Hand-on involvement returns blessing dividends that donations alone cannot match. Plus labor is part of our mandate.

Matthew describes Jesus' journey through towns and villages, healing, teaching, and proclaiming the good news of His kingdom. When Jesus sees the great number of people in need, Matthew tells us that, "He had compassion on them because they were confused and helpless, like sheep without a shepherd. He said to His disciples, 'The harvest is great, but the workers are few. So pray to the Lord who is in charge of the harvest; ask Him to send more workers into His fields'" (Matthew 9:36-38 NLT).

Notice that Jesus didn't say, "Pray to the Lord who is in charge of the financial reserves; ask Him to send more donations."

To take this a step further, token involvement is not what Jesus requested. Notice that He also didn't say, "So pray to the Lord who is in charge of the harvest; ask Him to send more workers into His fields so they can each occasionally pick one or two clusters of grapes." Workers worth their wages and their master's approval stay vineyard focused until the harvest is finished.

Gospel rescue mission leaders will tell you that they are inundated with offers from volunteers who want to pick one or two clusters—to serve on Thanksgiving or Christmas. They will also tell you that rare are the volunteers who want to serve a Monday supper in March or a Sunday breakfast in September. As one gospel rescue mission director stated, "While we are appreciative of all volunteers, regrettably, for many people, putting sweet potatoes on a plate during the holidays seems to be enough service to the poor to take the edge off any guilt they might feel for all they have and all they're getting at that time of year."

Same Kind of Different As Me (Thomas Nelson, 2006) tells the inspirational and emotionally gripping story of a homeless drifter and a high-end art dealer and his wife who connect at a gospel rescue mission in Texas. The couple, Ron and Deborah, started out serving an evening meal at the mission once a week. Deborah absolutely fell in love with the guests at the mission, calling them "God's people." She learned their names, birthdays, and life stories, and she convinced her husband that one evening a week wasn't enough.

Once a month, she instituted a "Movie Night," and then "Birthday Night," and then "Concert Night." During another innovation, "Beauty Shop Night," Deborah, enlisted the assistance of her best friend, Mary Ellen. Ron explains what transpired:

"They would go to the mission loaded down with makeup kits, hairstyling tools, perfume soaps, and every manicure and pedicure accessory ever invented. And the homeless women would come. Deborah and Mary Ellen would comb the lice out of their hair, then wash and style it with blow dryers and curling tools. If a woman wanted a pedicure, Deborah and Mary Ellen would wash her feet, use pumice stones to scrub away calluses layered on by ill-fitting shoes, and paint her toenails in a feminine shade of red or pink. They did facials and makeovers and gave the women little makeup kits to keep. Sometimes, on these nights, a homeless woman, catching a glimpse of herself in the mirror, would remember what she looked like before her life went off course and begin to cry."

Can you picture yourself serving in that kind of community, offering that kind of hospitality? Art dealer Don didn't initially, but the book tells the touching story of how the couple's increasing involvement with the poor changed their relationship with each other and their relationship with God. It changed many of the guests at the mission—including the homeless drifter, Denver—and changed the community. Despite their busy lives, they found that they couldn't afford not to be involved at that level with hungry, homeless, abused, and addicted people—their formerly invisible neighbors.

Christian social activist Shane Claiborne once stated, "Most good things have been said far too many times and just need to be lived." Nowhere is this truer than in the area of caring for poor people.

You can start right on your own street with those sometimes hard-to-detect invisible neighbors who may be on the verge of despair and ruin—like the elderly couple not making ends meet or the young couple just served foreclosure papers. Start with a visit; maybe take them a casserole or carryout. When you get to know them, invite them for coffee or supper. Let them know your home and heart are always open. Fill their car with gasoline. Pay a utility bill. Bring back a bag of groceries for them when you go to the market for yourself. Take them to the movies or a concert and remind them how to have fun. Introduce them to your friends of like faith and mind so the opportunity for mutual blessing can be shared. Invite them to be part of your small group. You don't have to be a highly esteemed spiritual leader or have everything in your life put together in order to bring them into community and administer hospitality. You just have to be available.

For the hard-to-neglect invisible neighbors—like the mother and child just surviving in their van—help them with a plan that allows them to see further into the future than they may be able to look right now. Help them find the social services they need. Take them to the gospel rescue mission. After you become well acquainted and have determined that they pose no safety risk to you and your loved ones, invite them to park in your driveway. Connect them with someone who has extra bedrooms and doesn't need the rent money. It might even be in your own house. North America's empty-nester baby boomers alone have enough spare bedrooms among them to dispatch short-term homelessness as it presently exists. We're just not used to living like people have to in many countries around the world, at least not yet.

For the easy-to-reject invisible neighbors—like those in dire straits or with addictions and mental-health issues who haunt skid row—partner with a gospel rescue mission where you can serve these people directly or indirectly. Missions can use your assistance on every level of their operation. For example, if you have business savvy, you might make a good board member. If you have the gift of administration, assisting with office work would be a valuable contribution.

Missions are always looking for people to bring conversation to the table—to talk to men, women, and families and make them feel welcome at the missions. There are plenty of opportunities to lead Bible studies. If you have counseling experience, that's an added bonus that can bless a mission.

Some missions have a youth center in the city or a camp in the country that utilize volunteers. In these settings, they work with young people who without direction are likely candidates to be mission residents. The emphasis is on building relationships and doing prevention counseling so that they don't have to do rehabilitation counseling later.

Of course, there are always volunteers needed to help with building maintenance, IT tasks, housekeeping chores, and kitchen work. That's where a lot of people—such as Ron, Deborah and Mary Ellen—start out so they can get a feel for what's going on. Another big need is for people to sort donations of clothes and household items that will eventually be passed on to guests or sold at a second-hand shop to cover mission expenses.

Each mission is unique; every mission is open to creative ways to serve. But go to serve others, not to feel better about yourself for offering.

A final word of caution: People with addictions and mental illnesses, or who have been hardened by years of living on the streets, can be manipulative and even dangerous. It takes training and experience to work with them successfully. Know your limits.

To locate a gospel rescue mission near you—or to get information about how to start one—go to the Association of Gospel Rescue Missions website, www. agrm.org. When you contact a mission, ask for the volunteer coordinator or the director of hospitality services. Then be prepared for God to use you and move you in ways you've never imagined.

## CONNECT

Why did Jesus ask His disciples to pray to the Lord of the harvest about sending laborers rather than just telling them to be the laborers? When was the last time you prayed about the sending of laborers as opposed to praying for the laborers who are already in the field?

What does it take for someone like Deborah or Mary Ellen to want to comb lice out of a stranger's hair? What would it take for you to do something like that?

When you consider the volunteer roles available at a gospel rescue mission, which one could you see yourself doing? How could your known spiritual gifts be exercised at a gospel rescue mission?

What was the occupancy rate* of your house or apartment last month? Is such a question too personal, even for a Bible study centering on homelessness? (*To determine occupancy rate, count the number of beds you have and multiply that number by the number of days in the month. This is your availability number. Next determine how many nights during the month each bed was used. Add the usage nights together. This is your usage number. Divide your usage number by your availability number to determine occupancy rate, or percentage of utilization.)

Could the area where you live use a gospel rescue mission (or an expansion of one that's already there)? Would the biggest obstacle be the availability of funds, the opposition of neighbors, or the fact that a mission would be in competition with local churches?

## GO DEEPER

As a group, make arrangements to spend a Saturday or Sunday afternoon and evening at a gospel rescue mission and take turns doing some of the jobs that need to be done. Talk to some of the guests about what they appreciate most about the mission. When you get back together, talk about your impressions and what you might be able to do to regularly help the mission.

ALTERNATE: Take a look at the programs two gospel rescue missions—one out west and one in the east—have developed to call attention to and do something about the tremendous need on the streets. Both of these programs also provide groups interested in learning more about the homeless with eye-opening perspectives. The first is called Sleepless. You can learn about it at http://www.invisibleneighbors.org/pages/links. The second is called My Night In a Box. Originally designed for students, groups of all ages are now participating in this program. Learn more at http://mynightinabox.com Think about putting on a Sleepless or My Night In a Box event in your area, to benefit your local gospel rescue mission, or to call attention to the need for one. Many have done so with amazing results.

# Part Three: Don't forget the words

Not long ago, I re-read a first-edition version of Through Gates of Splendor (Harper & Brothers, 1957) by Elisabeth Elliot. If you're not familiar with the work, it's the true story of five missionaries slain by the Auca Indians of Ecuador in January of 1956. Cultural anthropologists today would be quick to condemn the ideology and initiatives of European and North American missionaries of centuries past, but that's another story.

The book totally pulled me into a post-WWII Christian sub-culture that has now all but disappeared, half a century later. The author described the upbringing, scholastic achievements, conversion, and courting years of each martyr. As I read quotes from their diaries (which, I'm sure, they never supposed would be published), I was taken by their copious references to their faith, and their constant reciting of Scripture, spiritual poems, and old hymns. Other than a few erstwhile preachers I've heard on static-filled AM radio stations, very few people I know talk like that today—and I live in Colorado Springs, home to more than 100 Christian organizations!

Indeed, it was their burning desire to go and preach the gospel to the lost that drove Nate Saint, Jim Elliot, Pete Fleming, Roger Youderian, and Ed McCully together. It drove them to that fateful encounter on the Rió Curaray in the South American jungle.

Not long after reading Through Gates of Splendor, I came across a piece by Brad Greenberg in the "Houses of Worship" section of the Wall Street Journal. Called "How Missionaries Lost Their Chariots of Fire," it describes the significant swing in Christian missionary culture since the Eisenhower era.

Greenberg discusses how evangelistic fervor has diminished and how the emphasis in missions has changed. He submits that missionaries used to go overseas to preach about Jesus and make converts. "Christians today," he writes, "typically travel abroad to serve others, but not necessarily to spread the gospel." He suggests that the vast majority of them go to nations where Christianity is already known, to work for social justice and to expand their horizons or strengthen their spirituality.

As Greenberg explains this paradigm shift, he quotes David Livermore from Cornerstone University's Global Learning Center: "In a postmodern context, it goes against the grain to...do hard-core proselytizing. To millenials, it really feels like al Qaeda in Christian wineskins."

A professor from the missions department at Wheaton College added that two decades ago, half of his graduate students believed that building churches abroad was their leading objective. Fighting human trafficking, caring for AIDS orphans, and ending poverty are now the popular priorities. While these are indeed very worthy concerns, this shift has evoked some to question whether the message of the cross has become secondary to serving a cause.

What does all of this about foreign missionaries past and present have to do with invisible neighbors here at home? How does it relate to the ministry that you might do on your street or in a gospel rescue mission? There is a significant correlation.
As I talk to people across North America about the work taking place at gospel rescue missions today, I often hear things like, "I too want to preach the gospel by feeding the

hungry and housing the homeless." It's as if the very acts of hospitality are the essence of the gospel. To be clear, hospitality demonstrates the character of Jesus, but without the words of Jesus, the gospel is speculative rather than substantive. (See Romans 10:17.)

Without a doubt, there is an uptick in the attention religious people are paying to hungry, homeless, abused, and addicted people in our society. One reason is that current economics are a reminder that most of us are a few bad decisions or unfortunate circumstances away from being poor ourselves. But with so much to be done, it's easy to get caught up in doing only to find that we have marginalized the words we are called to proclaim.

Greenberg concludes his article with these words: "Spreading Christianity through deeds alone aligns with a quote attributed to St. Francis of Assisi: 'Preach the gospel always, and if necessary, use words.' But research suggests that non-Christians often miss the message without the words."

Said another way, these days, invisible neighbors "should not be expected to connect dots they may not even know exist." Fewer and fewer of the folks who live on your street or come to a gospel rescue mission have any biblical teaching. The "old, old story" needs to be told anew.

To be sure, I am not suggesting that preaching needs to precede hospitality initiatives. In fact, for a lot of people these days, premature preaching, delivered with the intent to convince or convict, is more of a deterrent than an enticement to Jesus and the message of His kingdom. Do the deeds, but don't forget the words. Just allow the Spirit of God to take the lead.

In a culture becoming increasingly paranoid of any proselytization, these lines from the apostle Paul to his prodigy Timothy can be pretty intimidating, but they are, nevertheless, our continuing mandate: "Preach the word; be prepared in season and out of season; correct, rebuke and encourage—with great patience and careful instruction" (2 Timothy 4:2).

We don't have to talk like the missionaries Nate Saint or Jim Elliot did—but we do have to talk.

What do we say? We tell our story. We tell Jesus' story. We talk about how the two stories are inextricability and everlastingly linked. Then we continue to care for invisible neighbors in a way that would cause no one to ever deny that what we say is absolutely true.

CONNECT

Throughout a typical day, what percentage of your conversations would you say are obviously spiritual in nature? Do you ever get the sense that you have to force yourself to talk about things related to Jesus?

Which missionaries, or people who have devoted their lives to serving others for the sake of the gospel—famous or not famous—have inspired you? Which of their traits or characteristics causes you choose them?

What is the best thing the proliferation of short-term missions has done to further Jesus' kingdom work? Could people who volunteer at a gospel rescue mission be considered missionaries, or is that a distortion of the term in your mind?

What is your favorite way to share your faith? Is it possible that what keeps some people from even attempting to share their faith is the assumption that they need to make converts in order to be a successful witness?

How exactly is your story and Jesus' story linked? What would it take to make that link much stronger and more obvious?

# SESSION SIX NOTES

# GROUP PRAYER & PRAISE SHEET

Briefly share your prayer requests as a group, recording the requests below. Remember to record any answers to prayer below.

| PERSON | PRAYER REQUEST | PRAISE RESPONSE |
|---|---|---|
| | | |
| | | |
| | | |
| | | |
| | | |
| | | |
| | | |
| | | |
| | | |
| | | |
| | | |
| | | |
| | | |
| | | |
| | | |
| | | |

# Epilogue: The world will be watching

Minding the gap, I got off the London Underground at Bank and walked up the steps into daylight. The six streets that converged in front of me were full of classic black cabs and red buses. I dodged them all, plus the puddles, and made it to Mansion House. At this official residence of the Lord Mayor, the London City Mission was holding its annual gathering of supporters.

On the other side of the security scanner, I was warmly welcomed and escorted to the lavishly appointed Egyptian Hall. The chamber was buzzing with distinguished Brits; my usher selected a few for introductions. Minutes later, a loud voice rose over the chatter announcing the processional of dignitaries, putting us all in our seats in silence.

During the next 60 minutes, I learned much about the historic London City Mission. In its early days, it was a powerful influence in making Members of Parliament and the general public aware of the terrible conditions in which many people were living in England's burgeoning capital city. The mission pioneered many of the methods of social provision and gospel outreach that have become the norm for the government and churches.

The mission still works with the marginalized. It now also ministers to people in hospitals and care homes, plus it provides chaplaincy services for railway and Tube workers, police officers, ambulance workers, taxi drivers, postal employees, and others.

But the one venture of London City Mission that seemed most intriguing was simply referred to as Ethnic Ministry.

London, you see, is a "global city" where 300 languages are spoken. Nearly two million London residents were born outside of the UK. London City Mission believes its role is to welcome these aliens, provide refuge, help them to be understood and find services, and introduce them to Jesus (see Mark 13:10). The UK church has never really rallied around this responsibility, and now, with church attendance in a virtual freefall, London City Mission is clearly in the lead in this regard. And the hospitality initiatives they are undertaking with hundreds of staff and volunteers—many of which are bilingual—are quite fascinating. They want no one to be invisible.

A look at what's going on in London provides two clear insights. The first is that cities and towns will continue to grow and be infused with differing cultures. Essentially, what this means is that the world is on its way to your door. For those who live in first- and second-tier cities, it's already there.

In Triumph of the City (Penguin Press, 2011), Edward Glaeser explains, "In the richer countries of the West, cities have survived the tumultuous end of the industrial age and are now wealthier, healthier, and more alluring than ever." People want to be where there is a chance for prosperity, and they are moving to places like London, and across the pond to cities from Miami to Vancouver. Glaeser adds, "Despite the technological breakthroughs that have caused the death of distance, it turns out that the world isn't flat; it's paved."

Confirming this, World Resources Institute says that the world's urban population is currently increasing four times as fast as its rural population, and projections show that by the year 2025, two-thirds of the world population could be living in cities and towns.

In this migration, original cultures are not being left behind.

Recently, I was in California and rode with a gospel rescue mission president from his administration building to his warehouse. In a span of 12 blocks, we passed through four different African "countries." Signage, restaurant aromas, and traditional native dress all told us when we had crossed another "border."

North America is no longer the melting pot; politics and progress have turned down the intense heat required to produce a consommé. What we now have is a pot of lumpy porridge. Unique cultural clumps simmer in a broth seasoned with resistance toward Western points of view and religious persuasions, giving off an exotic aroma. We have to get used to the fact that global cities are the future.

But the second insight from London—really, a confirmation—was that the gospel of Jesus, when served with generous hospitality, cuts through cultural differences and creates real neighbors like nothing else can.

Netravati moved from India to Shepherd's Bush in London's western suburbs. Folks from the London City Mission arrived only hours later. They brought her homemade nankhatai. Their decorated welcome kit included familiar spices from her native Kerala, tea, soaps, Type-G electrical plugs, a map marking many of the places they thought she would frequent, a pass for the Tube, the business card from a respected Indian physician, and phone numbers and email addresses of her new London City Mission neighbors. One in particular, Leslie, stopped to see her twice a week to make sure she was getting along in greater London. In three months, her visits went from hellos at the door to long conversations over tea.

I met Netravati at Mansion House. She told me, "When I got to London, I quickly found others living around me who had also moved from India. It was comforting because we shared a common past. But the mission people were different. At first I thought they wanted things from me. I later realized they wanted things for me. They wanted me to know a community of love and to experience peace in my new surroundings. They wanted me to know a God of love who sacrificed everything for me. I may share a common past with my Indian friends, but with my mission friends, I share a common future."

As you put down Invisible Neighbors, I pray that you pick up an enduring desire to serve the hungry, homeless, abused, and addicted—and also the aliens in your cities and towns. I don't believe it is pretentious to suggest that in the days ahead, all eyes will be on those who relentlessly demonstrate their commitment to Jesus by providing tender treatment to those who they know can provide nothing in return. And in fact, with the way things are going, you could even say that the world will be watching.

Here are a dozen things to do to inspire you to keep looking for and helping your invisible neighbors.

1. Write a document declaring your desire to be a "Matthew 25" individual, family, or group. Detail what that will mean and commit the points to memory. Hold a ceremony to celebrate the signing. Frame a copy and hang it in your kitchen or family room.

2. Learn who's on your street. Knock on some door that you rarely see open and introduce yourself. Organize and host a block party. Let people know they are welcome to stop by your place without an invitation.

3. Spend some time online and discover your city or town's demographic makeup. Learn what programs your local government is offering or proposing for the care of homeless people. Learn the locations where various social services are provided. Put everything on a map and keep it in your car.

4. Start a hospitality department at your church. Expand the definition of hospitality to include services for hungry, homeless, abused, and addicted people, and also aliens. Declare a Hospitality Sunday or Hospitality Month and bring in special speakers and artists.

5. Connect with the gospel rescue mission in your city, or the one closest to you. Get to know the staff. See what their volunteer needs are, and go and be blessed as you bless others. If there isn't a gospel rescue mission close to you, assess the need and talk to the Association of Gospel Rescue Missions (AGRM) about starting one. AGRM has a person who provides support for start-up missions.

6. Give financially to a gospel rescue mission or another ministry that is meeting the needs of hurting people. Become a regular donor and encourage others to do the same.

7. Help organize a "Sleepless" or "My Night In A Box" event in your city or town. Information about these two ready-made awareness events can be found on the DVD that accompanies this book. Be sure to coordinate the event with the local gospel rescue mission.

8. Make it a point to study a new culture or sub-culture every month. Start with those who have an enclave close to you. Learn about their history, social mores, cultural faux pas, and predominant religions. Try their food. Get to know people from within that culture, share a meal with them and listen to their stories.

9. Work on developing an eye for street people by befriending several. Take them for coffee or to breakfast. Let them know where you stand on things like handouts, addictions, and your faith. Learn from them so you can have a good idea who on the streets is in need of what services, who might be a runaway, who is likely being abused, and who is playing the system. Be an advocate for all of them.

10. Convert a small room or large closet in your home into a mini-warehouse for those in need. Stock it with blankets, coats, hats, gloves, shoes, socks, first-aid supplies, eyeglasses, protein bars, nonperishable food items, coupons, Bibles, and anything else that you find is in high demand. Turn part of your car trunk into a mobile mini-warehouse and distribute the goods whenever you see people in need.

11. Get comfortable with having guests in your home. Start with a high school foreign exchange student or a young person attending your local college who can't afford a dorm room. See where it progresses. Dedicate a room to "angles unaware."

12. Pray for the invisible neighbors you start to see—remembering them by name as you learn who they are. Ask God to guard you against prejudices and resentment, and teach you through the disappointments and heartbreaks that always accompany ministry to broken people. Ask God to keep you mindful of your own brokenness and His wholeness, and tell Him that you simply want to be a clean pipe through which His message and blessings can flow.

## TO GIVE OR NOT TO GIVE

If you are unsure about what to do when you encounter a homeless person asking for assistance, you're not alone. Some people give pocket change as a way of "buying themselves out" of an uncomfortable situation. Some give money, hoping the person will do the right thing with the cash. Others shake their heads or mumble a "no," irritated at feeling accosted.

Many, not knowing what to do, pretend they don't notice and pick up their pace; or they keep their windows up and increase the volume on their dashboard CD player. None of these are ideal responses.

Sooner or later, you will encounter a homeless person on the sidewalk, or, at an intersection, you will pull up beside someone out of work, holding up a sign. When that happens, here are some things to consider.

**1. Be prepared.**
Anticipate the opportunities you will have to engage with another person and be "salt and light." Develop a game plan. In time, you might find that you are intentionally walking closer to the person on the sidewalk or merging into the left lane, just to ensure you have an encounter.

**2. Acknowledge the person.**
Simply acknowledging homeless people as human beings and taking the time to talk to them in a friendly, respectful manner can go a long way. Treat them no differently than someone else you casually meet on the street or for a get-together. Linger for a moment and talk. Becoming homeless can be very isolating, discouraging, and embarrassing; remember that we all need the consistent love and encouragement of other human beings to help us make smart choices in our lives.

**3. Recognize that homeless people (and their problems) are not all the same.**
The person you meet may be a battered woman, an addicted veteran, someone who is lacking job skills, or an individual facing another seemingly insurmountable challenge. Encourage the person to get help through a gospel rescue mission, but remember it's ultimately his or her decision. Gospel rescue missions offer immediate food and shelter, and many offer job training and long-term rehabilitation programs that deal with the root causes of homelessness.

**4. Don't give money.**
For many people, panhandling is their livelihood. And more often than not, they are panhandling for something you don't really want to support with your money. However, if the Holy Spirit of God makes it clear to you that money is needed in a particular situation, give responsibly.

**5. Provide an alternative to money.**
If the person is asking for food, instead of giving money, give McDonald's or Subway coupons. They are generally inexpensive and easy to carry. Better yet, bring carryout from a restaurant and sit or stand with the person and share it. Depending on the person's expressed needs, you can also offer gloves, socks, tissues, a granola bar, bottled water, and the like. Refer him or her to an agency that can provide food and shelter. Meeting the actual need is always better then giving money.

**6. Hand out business cards of people at the local gospel rescue mission.**
Go to your gospel rescue mission and find out which caseworkers are happy to have their contact information circulated on the streets. Carry a stack of their cards in your briefcase or handbag. If business cards aren't available, simply print up slips of paper with the mission's name and address, and the name of a contact person at the mission. If your church is well versed in helping hungry, homeless, abused, and addicted people, you can provide that information, as well. During daylight hours, you might consider accompanying the person to the mission or your church and personally introduce him or her to the folks.

**7. Don't hesitate to call the police.**
It's not uncommon for homeless people to find comfortable, out-of-the-way locations to congregate—under the end of a bridge, on a grassy flat near the creek bank, by a certain fountain in the park—and then adopt them as their habitat. After passersby get used to seeing them in these locations, they seldom take the time to observe movement. Be on the lookout. When it's very cold or very hot, a stationary individual might be on the verge of hypothermia or a heat stroke. Don't ever hesitate to go over and check on a homeless person. When in doubt regarding someone's condition, call the police. You might just save his or her life.

**8. Pray.**
As you see people in need, ask God to bring them peace and encouragement that day. Ask God to meet their physical and emotional needs, and to satisfy their spiritual hunger. And specifically ask God what He would have you do in each situation.

# ADDITIONAL RESOURCES

### CHURCH RESOURCE TOOLS
(bulletin shells, inserts, banners)

www.InvisibleNeighbors.org/pages/tools

### MORE INFORMATION ON THE ISSUES
(recommended books, videos & articles)

www.InvisibleNeighbors.org/pages/books

### ASSOCIATION OF GOSPEL RESCUE MISSIONS
(to find a rescue mission in your area)

www.AGRM.org

### ABOUT CROSSSECTION
(other church resources and campaigns)

www.Crosssection.com

## About the Author

John Ashmen, president and CEO of the Association of Gospel Rescue Missions, has spent 30-plus years in association management and executive leadership. He holds a bachelor's degree in Bible with a social work emphasis, and a master's degree in organizational management. John's writings have appeared in numerous books and journals and on websites, and he teaches college courses and ministry management seminars at home and abroad. He serves on the board of the City Mission World Association and the Christian Hospitality Network. John and his wife, Judi, reside in bustling, beautiful Colorado Springs, Colorado. Their grown children live in New Jersey, Sweden, and Tennessee.